Living Without Losing

Living Without Losing

Don Polston

HARVEST HOUSE PUBLISHERS
Eugene, Oregon 97402

Except where otherwise indicated, Scripture quotations are taken from the New American Standard Bible.

Living Without Losing

Copyright © 1975
Harvest House Publishers
Eugene, Oregon 97402

Library of Congress Catalog Card Number 75-27142
ISBN 0-89081-623-9

Printed in the United States of America

DEDICATION

To my Dad, Chester Polston, who

. . . exemplified the winning life

. . . loved me at all times

. . . had the secrets of success

. . . led me to Christ

. . . taught me to pray

. . . left his dying words with us—"Have peace within yourself and love one another"

. . . is in the presence of our Lord.

—his son, Don

CONTENTS

FOREWORD

One of the greatest thoughts I've heard is "You are the same today you'll be five years from now except for two things: The people you associate with and the books you read."

Don Polston has associated with the best, read the best, and here is the best of many books and lives digested by a man who has lived the principles.

Don is a practitioner not a theorist so his words will be worth thinking on and reading many times.

Whenever you open the book you'll find encouragement from the heart of one who has set great goals and exceeds them. He has done this with people, reproducing himself and his family life proves that a builder's family life does not suffer if you practice God's Laws.

I thank God for Don Polston's tremendous life and I'm tremendously proud to introduce him to you.

Charles "T" Jones

PREFACE

Every heart will vibrate to its own music. Like calls like! Each of us has his own needs, desires, goals, and aspirations. Whoever can speak to your needs, desires, and aspirations is your best friend. If your heart is tuned to the message of this book—you are ready. If not, lay it aside and wait for greater growth.

The title for the living drama found in the pages of this book came out of the life of Sir Winston Churchill. He was asked to speak before a group of schoolboys at Harrow, his old school. The master teacher told the boys to be prepared with pencil and paper to make sure they copied every word of the old statesman. Sir Winston Churchill was, at this time in his life, about 75 years of age. The day came when the Prime Minister of Great Britain was to speak. He stood, lowered his glasses to the end of his nose, shoved his fingers in his vest pocket (as was his custom), and said with great feeling, "Never give up! Never give up! Never give up! Never! Never! and sat down. His speech was over, but history had a new start.

This is my purpose for you. If you never, never, never, never give in you can build your own world! Happy building!

Thank you, Mrs. Jean Cowger, my faithful secretary, for the typing and retyping of this message. To all others, around the world, who through their books, talks, prayers, and thoughts have helped me to compile this book, I say "Thank you!"

—*Don H. Polston*

1

TIPS FOR TRIUMPH

But thanks be to God! For through what Christ has done, he has triumphed over us so that now wherever we go he uses us to tell others about the Lord and to spread the Gospel like a sweet perfume.

II Corinthians 2:14 TLB

Beware of judging your future within the limitations of the present.

Everything can change in one day by meeting the right person. Pray that you will be at the right place, at the right time, to meet the right person, so that together you may help one another.

Have you begun to assume that things will never be better? Then turn around and assume for a moment that everything might be possible. For the moment start assuming that things can be changed.

Life has intended that you succeed. Anything you need, God can help you provide. "I would rather attempt to do something great and fail," says Robert Schuller, "than attempt to do nothing and succeed."

As you are being led along the lines of triumph, remember to ask for a stronger back and not for lighter burdens. People who triumph are people who have developed muscles for added responsibilities.

Each triumph leads to a greater need for involvement. It is impossible to be isolated and involved at the same time. Isolation may be well for the weak but it is a poor place for the strong. Practice getting into the mainstream of things daily—get out where the action is. The better you know the action, the better you are geared for the reaction.

People will follow a leader. It is assumed that a leader is at the head of the line—not *showing* the way but *leading* the way.

People don't need a signpost; they need a leader. A signpost only tells you what is ahead, but a leader shows you how to get there.

All motivated groups have one motivated person at the top. He has an excitement of winning which is passed down to the very last person. Here are 4 tips for triumph: (1) For greater motivation, plan larger projects in shorter periods of time. This will put pressure on you for achievement. Each time you complete a project in the allotted time you will be educated for greater endeavors. (2) Don't substitute movement for results. Remember, you are after achievement! (3) Work, pray, and plan to win! Once you know His mind, never let it enter your mind that you can't win. Winning is a result of your planning. (4) If you are not winning, change your plans. You are not committed to a set of plans. If they fail, create others that will succeed.

There is no possible way to success without some opposition, setback, or personal loss, so you must take these and build on them. The platform of success is built from the broken boards of failure.

The strength of a man is not what's around him but what's in him.

The clue to your potential is your attitude toward setbacks. Show me the one who lets defeat and failure teach him wisdom and I'll show you someone who's a winner.

Being licked is valuable, if you gain wisdom from it. Cash in on your blunders. Turn your losses into gains by learning from each of them. Above all else—don't judge your future within the limitations of the present.

PRAYER: "Heavenly Father, because of Your love, I come to you. Because of Your love, I am eager for change in my life.

Thank You for the sense of excitement that wells up within me as I think on Your Name. Don't allow me to be a robot but challenge me to excellence because of love. In Christ's Name. Amen."

*Part of my
answer to prayer
comes through
my concerned attitude
because I am
God's "feeling agent."*

2

THE MAN OF GOD

For though you made him lower than the angels for a little while, now you have crowned him with glory and honor. And you have put him in complete charge of everything there is. Nothing is left out.

Hebrews 2:7, 8a TLB

The man of God does not count noses, nor does he operate through majority votes, when principles are at stake. He is a man filled with God, a man who speaks for righteousness and stands with an unpopular minority if that's what it takes.

The man near to the heart of God does not deny a single individual the right of private judgment. He generously allows other men their right of personal opinion, but he gives no place to false views of his fellowman or slights about the person and work of Christ.

The man of God knows nothing about "group thinking" or the "collective mind." He lets every man be a bishop in his own soul, answerable to God alone.

The man of God may be a victim of political maneuvering and slanderous plots, but he commits his case to God and awaits vindication, though he be compelled to pass through the furnace of testing.

The man of God is not for sale. He cannot be silenced with gold, is not frightened by prestige, and does not quit when the going is rough.

The man of God walks with the approval of God in his soul,

the sunshine of heaven's triumph in his face. He thinks tall, speaks clearly, works hard, lives sacrificially, and sings in the midst of difficulty.

The man of God is a strong man, a Christ-man, filled with compassion for the straying, concern for the willful, and hate for sin on all levels.

The man of God speaks the truth, loves the truth, stands for the truth, and is ever ready to defend the truth. He never asks of a proposition, "Is it popular?" Only, "Is it right?"

The man of God is a sure foundation in the midst of a world of uncertainties. He is a defense against falsehood, a voice crying in the wilderness, "Make way for our God."

Every born-again believer is God's man. He is "bought with a price." What a price! It is not silver and gold, but the precious blood of Christ. He is a torch lighting the way for others to follow. He is a signal showing the way when it's dangerous.

The man of God is a man among men. Women respect him. Men lean on him. God trusts him. Oswald Smith said, "To get His best we must give Him our best. To win we must surrender. To live we must die. To receive we must give." Are you a man of God?

PRAYER: "Lord Jesus, You are the foremost thought in my mind today. I acknowledge Your power and ability to change my life. By faith I open my heart and mind to the Holy Spirit. Remove that which is undesirable, and intensify those things within me which are pleasing in Your sight. In the Name of Jesus. Amen."

If I have
received by faith,
I have truly received,
and the proof of
my having done so
is constant thankfulness.

3

HOW DO YOU TURN A MINUS INTO A PLUS?

I am with you; that is all you need. My power shows up best in weak people.

II Corinthians 12:9 TLB

Dr. Alfred Adler, one of the world's greatest psychologists, declared, "One of the wonder-filled characteristics of human beings is their power to turn a minus into a plus." All of you have read the old saying, "When you have a lemon, make lemonade out of it." The "born loser" (and there are none!) does just the opposite. If he finds life has handed him a lemon, he gives up. He has a dark feeling that fate is against him, that he doesn't have a chance. The person with lemons—infirmities and handicaps—can either build a successful life because of them or destroy his life because of them. One great man said, "I take pleasure in my infirmities." The wise person seeks to learn, to grow from his misfortune and turn it into his fortune.

2500 years B.C. the Greeks said, "The best things are the most difficult." Success is not mostly pleasure, it is mostly achieving. The great wonder of success is to turn the impossibility into reality. It is when the dropout becomes involved, the underprivileged becomes productive, and the defeated bounce back for another round in the ring of life. It does not take much stamina or intelligence to win when all is on your side, but it does take courage when it seems everything is against your fondest dreams.

Once you start to tackle the impossible, which you believe can be conquered, it is amazing how energy and enthusiasm quickly follow that decision. The person who wants to win always capitalizes on his losses. Say to yourself, "When I am weak, then am I strong."

Neitzsche said, "The superior man is not only able to bear up under necessity, but to love it." Many times it is heartache which is the spur that drives the loser to become a winner.

William James, the famous Harvard professor, proclaimed, "Our very infirmities help us unexpectedly." I feel sorry for the person who has it all. He will never know the joy of success. True success is getting it when it seemed impossible, doing it when there wasn't a ghost of a chance. Milton wrote poetry in blindness. Beethoven composed the "5th Symphony" when he was deaf. Abraham Lincoln became President of the United States when he was defeated more than 13 times for governmental jobs. George Washington Carver became world-famous in his scientific understanding of the peanut, even though his skin was black. This all spells success. It is turning the minus into a plus.

If you feel life has handed you a lemon, turn it into usefulness. Who knows, you may succeed far beyond your dreams. What have you to lose? Try it by the help of God and you may just turn your minus into a plus. Charlie "Tremendous" Jones declares, "The key is not planning [only] but it's 'Flexible Planning.' It is the ability to turn a minus into a plus by being ready with 'an alternate plan.' If things go wrong, plan your way to succeed with another, alternate plan."

PRAYER: "Heavenly Father, today, by the power of Your Word, I take my rightful place in life—that of dominion over principalities and powers. Through Jesus Christ I am able to live above problems and their causes, to respond in love to all who touch my life. I can develop my potential through Jesus Christ. Amen."

There is someone,
somewhere, sometime
who will help you
fulfill your dreams
and get
your prayers answered.

4

THE BIBLE—THE WORD OF GOD

The Lord God of Israel says, "Write down for the record all that I have said to you."

Jeremiah 30:2 TLB

The Bible reaches out beyond space, out beyond the rim of time, out into the stretches of eternity. In a thousand languages it speaks to men on every continent. It speaks the same message of hope to the heart of the savage and the cultured, gives to each the same warnings against willful disobedience to its laws. But to the despairing it offers hope and immortality to earthborn mortals. Wherever it goes it produces the same results—lifting, inspiring, enabling man!

The Bible is the record of God's approach to man, not man's attempt to find God. It is the record of a revelation of God to man and not the record of man's progressive discovery of God. Thus, "Holy men wrote as they were moved by the Holy Spirit."

Christians everywhere agree in declaring the work of the Bible and affirming their love for it. Nevertheless, the Bible is a closed book to many. By that I do not mean they do not understand it. I mean it is closed; it is seldom opened. Its pages are not read; its message is not sought; its teachings are received secondhand.

Never was the Bible printed in more languages, and never were there as many good versions in everyday language as today. Yet thousands of individuals, with the Bible on the shelf, live as though it did not exist.

The Bible is not to be worshipped or treated as a fetish; it is to be built into the lives of men. Its commands are to be obeyed, its Saviour worshipped and served, its teachings proclaimed to the ends of the earth. It will change social order as its principles become the warp and woof of the structure of society.

There are men who quote from the Bible to give weight to their arguments but by their lives deny its plain teachings. There are those who declare that the Bible should be taught in the public schools yet do not teach it to their own children.

Let all know that the Bible is the proclamation of the way of life. To disregard its teachings and repudiate its claims is suicide—to the intellectual, social, moral, and political being. To surrender to its Saviour, to live by its teachings, and to trust in its provisions is life—eternal life, abundant life, crowned with glory and honor.

Get your Bible open. Claim its promises, live by its commands, walk according to its rules, and you will enjoy the abundant life here and the glorious presence of God hereafter. Have you read your Bible today?

PRAYER: "Heavenly Father, You have told me that, having begun a good work within me, You will perform it until the day of Jesus Christ. I believe Your Word! By the authority of Christ, I claim that Promise for my own life. Continue to work within me. In the Name of Jesus. Amen."

*The Devil can have
no more power over you
than the thought
he can inject
into your mind.*

5

HOW TO HAVE A BETTER HOME

You wives, submit yourselves to your husbands, for that is what the Lord has planned for you ... husbands must be loving and kind ... children must always obey your fathers and mothers.

Colossians 3:18-20 TLB

Marriage is an investment that pays dividends, if you pay interest. Aurelius said, "The happiness of your life depends on the quality of your thoughts." Thoughts build or destroy homes.

The first home was in a garden; we know it as the Garden of Eden. God started man in an ideal environment; he had fellowship with the Creator, controlled all of the property, and knew all the animals by first name. Man walked freely beside its flowing rivers, freely ate much of its fruit, and kissed the first lady.

The home was God's first institution. He meant it to be a place of learning, growing, and sharing. But problems, heartaches, and hardships crashed into that first home and may crash into your home. If problems got into the first home, (when Adam and Eve fell to the deception of Satan) don't think your home will escape problems. The difference between a better home and an average home is that the better home knows how to handle its problems. Civilization has been built in the face of much difficulty, as every home must be built in the face of much difficulty.

24

One of the basic factors for better homes is better attitudes. A family's attitude is more important than the family budget. Attitude can change the budget, but the budget seldom changes the attitude. Husband is an attitude, then provider; wife is an attitude, then mother; sex is an attitude, then pleasure. All deep and meaningful relationships in the home are founded on correct attitudes.

Let's take a quick check on our attitudes in the home. Some-one said, "The man who wants to get somewhere should ride a winning horse." There's no better winning horse to ride than cheerfulness, a friendly and cooperative attitude in the home. There is not a man reading this book who wouldn't come home each night, on time, if he would find this kind of attitude waiting at the door. Robert Schuller affirms, "The wife can be her husband's biggest booster. Nothing is more important than building his ego—nothing is more disastrous than neglecting to boost, bolster, and build his ego." He goes on to say, "No man will ever leave or stop loving a positive-thinking wife who feeds his enthusiasm and self-confidence." But, hold on there before you say, "Amen," for there isn't a woman reading this who wouldn't give her all to find this same attitude coming through the door. Ask yourself, "Am I cooperative in my family?" "Am I fun to live with?" "Am I more concerned about the rules of the home than the romance in it?"

When was the last time you surprised the whole family with love and an expression of appreciation? Marriage is an invest-ment. It does pay dividends if you will pay a little interest. Invest tonight in your family and watch the dividends pour in tomor-row.

PRAYER: "Heavenly Father, You are the hope on which I can set my life; the foundation for a happy home. Today I ask that You would revive me within my home, do a new thing through me. Help me to portray the real picture of Christ to those with whom I live so I may rightfully reach out to touch my neighbor's life. In Christ's Name. Amen."

*Nothing in you
that has not died
will ever be raised
from the dead.
Nothing that you
have not given away
will ever be really yours.*

6

THE TEST OF A MAN

You husbands must be careful of your wives, being thoughtful of their needs and honoring them as the weaker sex. Remember that you and your wife are partners in receiving God's blessings, and if you don't treat her as you should, your prayers will not get ready answers.

I Peter 3:7 TLB

William Cowper Braun said, "The place to take the test of a man is not the forum nor the field; not the marketplace nor the Amen corner, but at his own fireside. There he lays aside his mask and you may judge whether he be imp or angel, king or cur, hero or humbug."

Braun goes on to say, "I care not what the world says of him, whether it crown him with honors or belt him with eggs; I care not what his reputation nor religion may be; if his babies dread his homecoming, and his better half has to swallow her heart every time she has to ask him for a shekel, he is a fraud of the first order, even though he prays night and morn until he is black in the face and howls, 'Hallelujah' until the eternal hills shake with sound.

"But if his children rush to the front gate to meet him, and loves own sunshine illumines the face of his wife when she hears his footsteps, you may take it for granted that he's true gold, for his home is a heaven. I can forgive much in that fellow mortal who would rather make men swear than women weep; who would rather have the hate of the whole he-world than the contempt of his wife, who would rather call anger to the eyes of a king than fear to the face of a child." This is the test of a man.

The word to the wise is, *"And you husbands, show the same kind of love to your wives as Christ showed to the church when He died for her" Ephesians 5:25 TLB*. The Bible also says, "You husbands must be careful of your wives, being thoughtful of their needs and honoring them as the weaker sex. Remember that you and your wife are partners in receiving God's blessings, and if you don't treat her as you should, your prayers will not get ready answers" (I Peter 3:7 TLB).

The test of a man is whether he does or does not repay evil for evil. His strength is seen when he doesn't snap back at those who may say unkind things to him, even in his home. He is learning to keep control of his tongue, especially around the house. Daily he seeks to turn away from evil and do good. He earnestly desires to live in peace at home and at work. He is known as a peacemaker wherever he goes. In this man's heart there is a conviction that the Lord is working with him and watching over him while leading his home to peace and prosperity.

The test of a man never ends! Of all the people on the earth, no one needs more strength, more love, and more encouragement than a man. If your score is low, fellows, ask God to give you a second chance—today!

PRAYER: "Precious Lord, thank You for Jesus. Through Him Your plan for redemption was made perfect; through Him I can say with assurance, 'Christ is in me'. Not because of anything I've done or deserved, but because I believe Your Word. Grow within me, Lord; teach me to share my life with those around me, especially my family. In Christ's Name. Amen."

*We do not pray
for faith
but seek to know God
and then
faith comes naturally.*

7

COMPLIMENTS CURE

So encourage each other to build each other up, just as you are already doing.

I Thessalonians 5:11 TLB

One of the basic needs in the human heart is for praise. I believe unrestrained compliments from members of the home to one another can heal any difficulty in the family. There is only one way to develop the "complimentary complex" and that is to forget yourself.

If the wife is afraid she may be taken for granted if she hilariously compliments her husband, she needs to remember that this is the secret of being remembered. Who can forget a complimenting wife? I have yet to see a man forget the woman who makes him feel great. The overflow from his heart back to her will make all other women burn with envy for a man like she has for a husband.

On the other hand, if the husband withholds his unrestrained admiration and love for his wife, she will die of "love malnutrition." But, if he forgets himself in both expression and experience of love, he will find he's living with a queen. Every man will look with pride on the wife of this loving man. Why is it that two people who are committed "till death us do part" fail to realize the high interest rate they both will pay on the uncomplimentary life?

Let's compare this to the church. The Bible tells us the husband is to love his wife as Christ loved the church. It also tells us that the wife is to respond (submit) to the husband as to the Lord. Now if the praise of the church honors the Lord and the overflow of Christ back to the church is love, doesn't it make sense that this formula can also work for home, too? When the church is praising her Lord, the Lord is loving His church.

If I were a woman, I think I would make it one of the highest goals of my life to praise and exalt my husband. Since I'm a man, one of the highest goals of my life is to love and please my wife.

Let the husband love, pursue, and remember his wife and she will, out of the overflow of her heart, praise and exalt him. If I understand the Scriptures correctly, the wife should be the reflection of the husband as the church is the reflection of her Lord. Praise glorifies the Lord, and compliments will build the image of the home. Your self-image will usually not be any greater than the image which you receive from your husband or wife. Compliment without a thought of reward, and watch the rewards come pouring back into your life!

I don't know any conflicts in the home that cannot be cured by sincere compliments. Compliments can heal your home.

PRAYER: "Lord God, I recognize You today as Saviour of my soul, and by faith I open my heart to the power of the Holy Spirit. Do a new thing in my life today. Warm my heart until loving and giving myself to others becomes a natural way of life. I believe You will do this in me. In the Name of Jesus. Amen."

Faith is fantasy,
unless it is made real
in the way
I interact with people.

8

HOW TO GET MORE THAN YOU GIVE

For if you give, you will get! Your gift will return to you in full and overflowing measure, pressed down, shaken together to make room for more, and running over. Whatever measure you use to give—large or small—will be used to measure what is given back to you.

Luke 6:38 TLB

Everyone knows if you want a field of corn, you need to plant bushels of seed. With every seed of corn, there is a possibility of 1500 seeds on an ear. If there were three ears on a stalk, you would have multiplied 1 seed into 4500 seeds. That's not a bad gain. There is only one way to get this kind of multiplication and that is by planting the living seed. This is what I call "seed sense." It is a sensible, businesslike venture to plant what you have harvested in order to gain a bigger harvest. Jesus said the same thing in Luke 6:38—"Give, and it will be given to you; good measure, pressed down, shaken together, running over, they will pour into your lap. For whatever measure you deal out to others, it will be dealt to you in return."

Many of us are poor because we don't give more. If you have a financial problem, start giving to others; if you have a psychological problem, start sharing yourself with others. This is planting seeds for a greater return. You'll always get more than you give. Are you planting money? Are you planting love? Are you planting hope?

I counsel with people who are always "up against it" financially, psychologically, and socially. They never seem to have enough to live the free and abundant life. Their idea is to keep all they make, both financially and socially. This attitude alone is enough to hinder all progress in their lives. When we assume the attitude of withholding any of God's gifts, our productivity and hope of prosperity become sterile. The abundant life is only for him who gives abundantly—both of himself and of what he possesses.

When you give to God, through men, God gives back to you, through men. Notice that the Biblical promise says that *they* (meaning men) will pour rewards back into your lap. Wealth that is shared is wealth that is invested. Invested wealth will bring a profit. There are forms of wealth that are not monetary. There is the wealth of understanding, love, hope, which we may share with others. The law of compensation operates as you invest these forms of wealth. The more you give—freely—the more abundantly it comes back to you—freely!

You are going to make money! You are going to invest yourself! You will get a greater return! Do not let time or pressure cause you to fall into doubt about these matters of investing and return. Resist all forms of doubt. Keep before you the principle, "Give and it shall be given unto you . . . again."

PRAYER: "Heavenly Father, Your Word says if I abide in You and Your Word abides in me I can ask anything in prayer believing and it will be reality in my life. Thank You for the power of a living Gospel. Teach me to apply Your Word to my life that it may glorify the Father and edify my fellowman. In the Name of Jesus. Amen."

*We are not fulfilling
our destiny unless we
are in a relationship
which is really
God living in us.
I must have
an experience so real
that God and I
are operating as one person.*

9

AMBITION

---

*This should be your ambition: to live a quiet life, minding your
own business and doing your own work, just as we told you before. As a result, people who are not Christians will trust and
respect you, and you will not need to depend on others for
enough money to pay your bills.*

I Thessalonians 5:11, 12 TLB

Someone said, "Ambition is the spur that makes man
struggle with destiny: It is heaven's own incentive to make purpose great and achievement greater."

The mysterious force which moves the human race onward
in its climb for excellence is ambition. Before the needle in a
compass will respond to the pull of the North Pole, it must be
magnetized. It can be made of the best of metals and ready for
use, but it will lie motionless until electrified by the mighty
magnet. Once it is magnetized, it will never be the same again.

Multitudes of people are like unmagnetized needles. They lie
motionless and unresponsive to the stimulus of faith. But, as
soon as the great and mighty magnet, Christ, touches them, they
will forever respond to the Star of Hope. The source of all
good ambition is a direct result of being magnetized by God.

Ambition is the gift of God. The constant inward promptings,
the earnest thrust of the mind is a divine gift. It is part of every
atom of the universe; it is the instinct of all forms of nature; it
is in the seed which is buried out of sight, pushing its way up
through the soil to produce fruit.

Without ambition, all of life is dull. If the creation would lose this Godward urge, everything would collapse, but when nature and man respond to this urge, there is hope and progress for all. That mysterious urge within us must be fed or it will die. Let no one hinder your ambitious urge. There is no limit to growth and development for you in this world.

When you reach one height of ambition, you will want to set goals for another. It will be like a divine impulse, pushing you on and on to greater goals. You have never heard of a man who strives faithfully and sincerely, with truth and faith, who fails to find his goal accomplished. Ambition is a gift of God to you. Use it or lose it!

The craving for something better is the best possible antidote for bad habits. Only those things which are fed tend to grow in our nature. The quickest way to kill them is to cut off their nourishment.

That inner call to go forward is God's voice—heed it! Jesus said, "I am the way, the truth, and the life. . . ." Only He can take your life on to usefulness as you hand it over to Him. Surrender to Christ and find the motivation for living.

PRAYER: "Heavenly Father, I'm thankful for Your complete love toward me—love that offers hope for achievement and excellence in my life. Give me the courage to cast off inferiority and lack and accept the challenge of change. In Christ all things are possible in my life. In His Name. Amen."

If you stand on the ground
of what Christ is,
you will find
all that is true of Him
is true of you;
but
if you stand on the ground
of what you are in yourself,
you will find
all that is true
of the old nature
is true of you.

10

PEACE OF MIND

*For the Holy Spirit, God's gift, does not want you to be afraid
... but to be wise and strong, and to love.*

II Timothy 1:7 TLB

We tend to become like our aspirations. If you really desire peace of mind, you can develop it. I use the word "develop" because you must change your thought pattern from worry to trust. If you feed the mind thoughts of unrest, you will grow a harvest of misery. Nothing strengthens the spirit like the spirit of peace.

Jesus said, "My peace I give unto you." Have you ever taken notice of the kind of peace Jesus had? Read the Gospels and you will discover that there is no greater peace of mind than what Christ had in all situations. Even on the Cross Jesus had peace of mind as He prayed for His enemies. He was able to commit Himself to God there on the Cross with perfect peace. Peace of mind is the greatest benefit to all of life.

Now don't expect that peace of mind will free you of problems—that's not the purpose. Difficulties are challenges to growth. If you seek to avoid difficulties to find peace of mind, you will only defeat yourself. The process of growing is the ability to handle problems peacefully.

Everything in life goes out of focus when you fail to maintain your peace of mind. A sign of maturity is peace in the midst of life when it is at full tide. Many are unable to meet life at full tide and have peace of mind. What you need to remember is that peace of mind can be part of living a full life. Peace comes from knowing you are doing your best at all times. It is a result of completed acts.

You will discover the principle of peace of mind as you seek to bring peace to others. When I turn my attention to myself, I usually lose peace. But when I turn toward others (even though I resist doing it at first) peace of mind and joy overwhelm me. At times a brisk walk in the night will restore peace of mind. Maybe if you would rearrange your room you would stimulate peace of mind. A change of scene at times brings temporary peace of mind, but keep it simple—don't fall into the death trap of spending money or buying things to maintain peace of mind.

The great things of life are free. The efficient mind is one which is at peace with itself, with others, and with God. The lasting peace for which all men are searching is found in Christ. When He removes all guilt and forgives sin, He also bestows peace to your soul. Peace is the result of respecting yourself, accepting God's plan for your life. Peace signs are on display all over the world, but true peace on earth and good will toward men is found in our Lord Jesus. Hand your life to Him. He can make something out of it peacefully.

PRAYER: "Heavenly Father, You said You would keep me in perfect peace if I would keep my mind stayed on You. Fill my life with that peace that I may praise You for doing something for me I couldn't do for myself. Now take me and set me apart to do Your will, always sharing what You have done in my life. In the Name of Christ. Amen."

*When we accept ourselves
instead of reject ourselves,
we accept others
instead of rejecting them.
We are the will of God.
We leave Him
to do the holding,
while we live normal lives.
We are His business.*

11

THE WINNING WIFE

If you can find a truly good wife, she is worth more than precious gems!

Proverbs 31:10 TLB

A woman is judged by many ideals: Is she tall, is she short, what about her figure, is she alert to her work, does she have sex appeal? I suppose the ideal could be a list as long as your arm. But the one great ideal of the winning wife is "Does she make her husband happy?" Now don't rush past that statement.

I counsel with hundreds of people who are unhappy. The majority of the counseling is with marriage-problem people. Both people can be good-looking, and both may seem to have a measure of adaptability. Both can have all that the other could expect—they come from good backgrounds and respectable jobs—but they are not happy. The husband looks inferior, he has a shameful complex about his whole person. The wife has weeping eyes and appears to be very insecure. It is very hard on the man's ego to seek my advice. It clearly shows that somewhere something has gone wrong in his family or between himself and his wife. He is a bit ashamed to openly recognize there is a problem. Both people are paralyzed. The wife is losing the battle, the husband has an ego that's undernourished. The whole thing is hung up.

It is my observation that when a man has to overpraise himself, it is usually because he is underpraised by the woman he loves the most—his wife. The most outspoken press agent for the husband should be his wife. Let her never fear she is overpraising him. Every man in the block will wish for the same response from his wife. The winning wife will become the envy of all women and men. You can keep your husband loving you forever by simply telling him he's wonderful, and by doing it sincerely.

Robert Schuller has found that, "A wife creates a positive mental element by being a cheerful, happy woman. Pity a man," he says, "who, tired from a day's work, has to come home to a depressed, fatigued, self-pitying woman! Be proud of your role as a wife and a homemaker."

"But, what if he isn't wonderful?" you say. There is no reason for him to be otherwise if you really think that. Who would know the difference if he changed when no one expects him to be any different? It is amazing how the magic of letting him glow under the wife's spotlight of admiration turns a man away from all the glitter of the age and sends him out to do the impossible and home to be the unbelievable. The next time you find your mate depressed or defeated, sincerely tell him, "You're the greatest!" It will turn the darkness of his mind toward the sunburst. The armor of leadership becomes tarnished unless it is polished by the praise of a woman. A praising wife can turn a failure to success, a fearful man to boldness. Remember, if he is winning in the struggle of life it can be related to the winning wife at home. All honors may go to him at the finish line, but when he reaches home, all the honors go to you. You make him a winner by being a winning wife yourself.

PRAYER: "Lord God, I see You today as a miracle God, able to reconcile my life unto Yourself. By faith I give up the right to myself and ask that You would reconcile my emotions, actions, and tongue unto Yourself. Make the things I do and the words I speak pure and totally pleasing to the image of Christ and to my God-given leader, my husband. In the Name of Jesus. Amen."

*We are a part of Christ
for others,
so we take a different
point of view in our
disturbing circumstances.
All life is now
an intercession.
We accept the unpleasant
situation as being from God
though apparently it is
from the Devil or man.*

12

I DARE YOU TO BE YOURSELF

Christ in your heart is your only hope of glory.
Colossians 1:27 TLB

You are likable, but do you know it? There are great qualities in you, hidden under the topsoil of fear. Your teachers told you what a misbehaved child you were; others reflected on your mental ability; and still others teased and tormented you about your looks, your background, or your aspirations. The greatest mistake of your life is that you accepted it all as gospel. You believe more in your weaknesses and failures than in your strength and your possible success. It is amazing how many people can forget their accomplishments but can't forget their mistakes. Many of us seem to feel the need to suffer, to fail or be miserable, because we have a sense of unworthiness.

Try liking yourself! You should be reminded that there is no other person like you. There is a quality, a personality, about yourself which is unique to society and to your world. That's the law of the universe. God has established this principle in all nature. Be yourself!

There was a time in my life when I wanted to be like my superiors. I wanted to preach like my pastor, dress as he dressed, and handle people as he handled people, until one day I discovered he was making more enemies than friends. I had the false idea that I should pray like Wesley, study like the mystics, and preach like Billy Graham. I thought I would offer to the world the most outstanding combination of all three in one. I thought this would bring me to instant happiness and success. It took me many years to discover this combination of personalities was a hindrance to my personality and a road-block to success.

I would spend whole nights awake thinking how I could speak better or perform more pleasingly to suit everybody, everywhere, at all times, hoping to give to them this rare combination of many men in one. The result was confusion to my mind, frustration in my spirit, and a sick and weary feeling in my chest. With this confused combination of personalities I nearly failed. It would have driven me out of public life, had I continued the false image.

One day it began to dawn on me—dare to be yourself! I had begun to say, "If people don't like who I am and how I do it, that's fine with me." I concluded that if society didn't like my southern drawl and my unique and quick way of phrasing ideas or my untraditional manner as a speaker, then just look what they're missing! Sounds egotistical, doesn't it? But, that's what saved me from a miserable breakdown. I had to decide to be myself, by the grace of God, and let the chips fall where they will. To my glad surprise, everything in life began to take on the image of success, joy, and achievement. Life had my thumbprint on it and I began to like the thumbprint. I have never been happier or busier in my life than I am today. Every day is fun now because I am bold enough to be myself. Humility is a matter of the heart. That is where I shall be judged. A famous psychiatrist said, "The self-image we harbor is the key to the success or failure of our most cherished plan and aspiration." I want you to start today to be yourself—improve your talents, your creativity, honesty, and sincerity. You will discover in time that the world has been waiting for your type. I dare you to be yourself—your best self! One of America's greatest motivators discovered, "We have become a nation of followers following followers who are following followers."

When you dare to be yourself you break away from being a "follower of the followers."

PRAYER: "Heavenly Father, I praise Your Holy Name with glory and honor. I willingly open my life to the control of the Holy Spirit. I lay aside my inferiority and confusion and ask that my mind be made whole by Your power. I accept the plan You have for my life, to do, to be, and to become all things to all men. In the name of Christ. Amen."

All life is making choices
and
choices make destiny.
I become what I choose.
The law of choice
is the same
as the law of faith.
What I take takes me.

13

WALK THROUGH THE OTHER DOOR

I have learned to be content in whatever circumstances I am.
Philippians 4:11 TLB

Have you read Dr. A. J. Cronin's novel, *Hatter's Castle*? When he was a doctor in London, on the verge of his greatest success, his health broke. He was told to take a year's rest and that he might never again be fit to stand the wear and tear of the medical profession.

What a blow! He loved his work. From a small and humble beginning he had achieved his life's objective, and now it must be abandoned. The door to a medical career was slammed in his face. He voiced bitterness and resentment to all of his friends. Life had turned sour.

While in exile in the West Highlands, time hung heavy on his hands. Hours felt like years; the door to success had been shut. Suddenly one day an impulse came to him to write, and he began the novel *Hatter's Castle*. When it was finished, it was packed up and sent to the publisher. To his glad surprise, it was accepted. Out of all reason, another door had opened to him. A whole new career of writing lay before him as he walked through "the other door."

Many of us, when meeting with sudden disappointment, misfortune, or defeat, raise a cry of anger and resentment against God and life. When we miss a chance of promotion or when we are deprived of good health, it is hard to understand.

49

We cry, "Why did this happen to me?" or "Why did God allow this to come into my life?" But we need to see that there is another door. The prophet Job had a hard time understanding his losses as well. In fact, Job's wife said, "Curse God and die." Her idea was, let's get on with it and let death overtake us.

It is more difficult to live than to die. However, we cannot measure divine providence by the yardstick of man's mentality. What we think is evil may well be for us an eventual good. The other door may be the very best one after all. Walk through it and find out for yourself. God says, "I have set before you an open door and no man can shut it."

Disappointments and trouble are often the instruments with which we are fashioned for better and bigger things to come. You must never give up. Life never takes away from us without giving something better in its place. Life is no straight and easy corridor; the road is not always smooth and unhampered. Many times our paths are like a maze of passages through which we must seek, search, and find our way. At times we find our way and then are confused—now a clear light to go, then checked by a red light to stop. At one time we find ourselves on a freeway and then again in a blind alley. But always—if we have faith—God will open another door. Perhaps not the door we thought was the best, but another door which He knows is the best, will take us to a greater and more useful destination. Out of my deepest hurts have come my greatest strength.

Robert Louis Stevenson said it well: "Give us the strength to encounter that which is to come, that we may be brave in peril, constant in tribulation, patient in all changes of life, and down to the gates of death loyal and loving to one another." If the door you hoped for has closed, try the other one—it just could be the pathway that could lead to the greatest fulfillment of your dreams.

PRAYER: "Heavenly Father, You are a great God, wise and loving. I recognize Your ability to change my life, Your concern and deep care for me as a unique individual, and I feel thankful for Your love toward me. God, I want You to have complete control of my inner thoughts and outer actions. Take my life now, use it to glorify Your Name and to further the abundant life in Jesus Christ. In His Name. Amen."

There are 5 outlets of power:
  1) *What we are*
  2) *What we say*
  3) *What we do (service)*
  4) *What we give (money)*
  5) *What we pray*

14

THREE STEPS TO SUCCESSFUL LIVING

You will also decree a thing, and it will be established for you.
Job 22:28 TLB

There isn't any situation so hard that if you chipped away at it long enough you couldn't create a monument. Monuments are usually created out of hard situations.

I was conducting motivation seminars in Rapid City, South Dakota, when someone suggested I visit Mt. Rushmore. I had never seen the famous faces. As my wife and I approached the mount, I first got a glimpse of Washington's face through the tall, towering trees. There it was—strong, beautiful, and mammoth. When we reached the foothills we stood listening in wonder and amazement to the history of this unique creation. Someone had chipped away long enough in the hard granite to create this soul-moving experience.

Below the magnificent faces were the chips, millions of them. I said, "This is the secret of success. Keep chipping away at your granite until you produce your project." If you know what you're after, don't let anything cause you to quit.

But before one can create a monument, he must make use of three steps of success: (1) Daily "visualize" yourself in the completed project. What can you see? Nehemiah wanted to rebuild the old walls around Jerusalem. Surrounded by rubbish, Nehemiah could visualize strong walls. In fact, his enemies asked the question, "Will they revive the stones out of the heaps of the rubbish?" See yourself in the completed project.

(2) You must "verbalize" your objective to yourself. You will be surrounded by doubt and negative attitudes daily as you seek to unfold your life's ambition. Through "verbalization" you will establish in your mind the object you really want. Jesus said, "Say to this mountain, be thou removed. . . ." Again we are told, "Decree a thing and it shall be established unto you." The next time you are tempted to speak words of defeat, remember, you will create the thing spoken. God spoke worlds into existence! (3) Practice daily the law of seizing it. "Vitalize" your vision. Act just as you would if you already had obtained it. Action breaks indecision. Assume the position and action you would if the desired project had already been completed. Do this until the demand of your vision is fulfilled. Everything you need to know and do will come to you. Your destiny is completely in your hands. Don't be afraid of changing your vision, vitality and self-image. People with a negative attitude toward change are giving themselves a message of death, a message which is hastening their separation from this world. For as the world becomes filled with the new and strange, they become strangers ready for the great departure. The keys to success are: see yourself as successful, and say to yourself each day what your idea of being a success is, and act your way to success.

PRAYER: "Lord God, Your Word says, 'Decree a thing and it shall be established unto you'. I believe Your Word and decree myself to be made whole in Jesus Christ. By His power I decree success as I lay my plans and carry them out with prayer and dedication. In You I am free to fulfill the great plan You have for my life. In the Name of Jesus I pray. Amen."

*The Holy Spirit
is at work in new ways
in every generation
and we are on tiptoe
for any participation
in these new ways.
He is always original
and may have some
original calling for us.*

15

HOW TO INCREASE YOUR ENERGY

Those who hope in the Lord will gain new strength; they will mount up with wings like eagles, they will run and not get tired, they will walk and not become weary."

Isaiah 40:31 TLB

The experts agree that many individuals, pushing their energies to the extreme, may in a vast number of cases keep up the pace day after day and find no bad reaction from it at all. Why? Because it has been proven that the busiest person needs no more hours of rest than the one who is idle. In fact a survey was taken which shows psychological fatigue to be predominant over purely physical fatigue with the busy person.

Boredom is the number one killer of increased energy. Dr. Warren Guild, of Harvard Medical School, says, "Chronic lack of energy is due to emotional factors and is likely to appear as soon as a person wakes up in the morning. Yet, if someone suggests doing something interesting, a person will often find he has enough energy to do it, even though exhausted a few minutes ago."

The best antidote to boredom, lack of energy and zest for living is to find something in life that is interesting to you and helpful to others. The Bible teaches, "They shall run and not be weary, they shall walk and not faint." That applies to the person who has found something stimulating and interesting in life.

It has been discovered that a chronic lack of energy among

women is often due to an unconscious conflict about what she wants out of life. She may feel a lack of energy to clean her house, prepare meals, and keep the clothes washed because her mind is in conflict with other projects which she may feel are more rewarding and creative than housework. We seldom lack energy to do the things we find interesting and challenging.

I was in Denver, Colorado, recently on my way to a motivation seminar. While waiting for my flight, my attention was drawn toward an old man, perhaps 80 years of age. He walked with abounding energy. He talked to the stewardess with enthusiastic tones and had a shine on his face equal to any in the world. As the people assisted him with his luggage and the stewardess fastened his seat belt, I could hear his ringing voice above all the noise of the airport as he spoke in colorful words, "Thank you." I confessed to myself that the old gentleman had magnetism! Everyone loved him because he loved everyone with increased energy. I heard him say to one of the girls that he was on his way to visit a sick brother (probably a brother younger than himself!).

A lack of energy is the inability to attach excitement to a goal-directed activity. Laziness, chronic laziness, is the direct result of a lack of interest in a worthy project.

Develop worthy projects and goals, then watch increased energy pour into you. Discover something exciting in your job or in your home. Fall in love with a project and turn your lack of zeal to unlimited, creative energy. The secret behind energy that motivates is to love what you're doing! Seize opportunities that are ignored by others. Get excited about what you're doing today!

PRAYER: "Heavenly Father, I see the work of Your hands around me and I give thanks for being a part of Your plan. Today is a new day and a new experience. Expand my concept of life, that I might not miss what You hold in trust for me. I open my heart and am willing to receive all You have for my life. In the Name of Jesus. Amen."

*As intercessors
we are mouths without teeth,
arms without muscles,
if we have all the rest
but have not
the Word of authority.*

16

WHAT DOES IT MEAN TO BE A SELF-STARTER?

A joyful heart is good medicine, but a broken spirit dries up the bones.

Proverbs 17:22

What does it take to get you moving? It has been said, "Behind every successful man there is a surprised mother-in-law." Whatever there is which keeps you alert, alive, and moving is more valuable to you than any other single factor in life. There are some experts in behavioral science who teach that many men are motivated by a woman's love. In his motivation achievement a man is hoping to attract the woman he loves and gain her admiration and respect. Believe it or not, there is some truth behind that observation.

Historians seem to think Napoleon sought world leadership because of his love for his wife. He was conquering the world to conquer a woman. Who knows? But I do know the love of a woman can turn the tide in any man's life.

The fact remains that the self-motivator is usually a winner. A psychologist tells us, "The factor that makes for a self-starter is a desire to satisfy either (1) his self-esteem or (2) his own interest or (3) his conscience." This psychologist goes on to say, "Man not only wants the high regard of other people, but he also must have a high regard for himself. Once he sets himself on course, the self-starter proceeds energetically and with utmost confidence, having no intention of letting any obstacle stand in his way." It was St. Paul who said, "I can do all things through Christ who strengthens me."

Self-starters have been the pioneers in history.

What is the magic fuel in the self-starter which puts him among the winners? What is that little difference between people, when one has the inner engines running smoothly and the other has his inner engines rusting and wasting away? Some of the experts say the difference is in the fuel, such as the desire to acquire luxuries, or perhaps the satisfaction of personal ambition or money. For others, it is the desire to be leaders or to have public recognition.

The fuel for self-motivation includes, among other things: (1) financial security, (2) peace of mind, (3) freedom from fear, (4) hope for love, and (5) a desire to be among the winners. The self-motivator usually feels he is destined for greatness. It was Emerson who said, when hoping to ignite the motivation of men, "Do the thing and you shall have the power."

Death to the inner man comes from idleness without. If you are having trouble getting motivated, learn to keep in motion all day once you're started. Idleness is the sure path to destruction.

Dr. Karl Menninger, the noted psychiatrist, has said, "How long you live can very well depend upon your mental attitude. But, more important, how much you live depends almost wholly upon your mental attitude."

The optimistic, happy outlook of the self-motivator promotes energy, happiness, and usually good health. The depressed person slows down productivity, which affects his intake (financially) and his output. Doctors say his metabolism slows way down when he is unmotivated and will bring on sickness and other unhealthy reactions. "A merry heart does good like medicine, but a broken spirit dries the bones," said the prophet.

PRAYER: "Lord God, nothing is impossible through You. You are able to take a life without form and mold it into usefulness. Without You in control of my life, I remain stagnant and without a vision. I'm not willing for that. Motivate my life to achievement. Put within me a desire to excel in every area, that I might be useful in Your work. In the Name of Christ. Amen."

*We should expect God
to indicate His will
through our minds
and desires because
"we have the mind of Christ,"
and
"it is God who is at work
in you, both to will
and to work
for His good pleasure."
So we must not
be afraid of our thoughts.*

17

A PRESCRIPTION FOR SUCCESS UNLIMITED

But seek first His kingdom and His righteousness, and all these things shall be provided for you.

Matthew 6:33 TLB

Observe carefully the things I'm about to tell you. If you follow my prescription for success exactly, you will find success and fulfillment each day of your life.

But to do this you must decide what you want. What is the success which you desire to gain, and can you gain it honestly?

In the first place you cannot depend on your intellect only to reach your goal of satisfaction. Why? Because the hard intellect insists on facts, figures, and cold reason. It sees only the difficult things to overcome. The outer mind is not interested in satisfaction, only in the situation. It gets full direction from the circumstances, obstacles, and problems. This is the reason success or happiness seldom come to the person who follows the impulses of his outer mind. The outer mind only works on the surface of things.

The tendency of the outer mind is to be blue and depressed, to see only the negative. The ability to see through the problem or obstacle to the solution is impossible while the outer mind has control. The outer mind says, "When all the facts fit, then move." It must be wholly convinced beforehand or it will not proceed. The brakes are half on most of the time when you are governed by the outer mind.

The inner mind functions not by cold logic, but assumes the attitude of accomplishment long before it is reality. Satisfaction and security are the evidences of your using the inner mind. It knows the need is the only authority for fulfilling its desires. If your deep inner feelings call for reality, follow them! But you must determine what you want!

Every achievement calls for greater opportunities. Success is unlimited if you have the unlimited patience to keep unfolding the blueprints of your deepest desires.

If you remember only the times of failure, embarrassment, and inability to function harmoniously, you only recall that which functions with the outer mind. You acted and spoke from what you could see, hear, and touch—not from what you sensed deep within. Avoid all performance which sees only the surface of things. Listen to your inner mind, ignore the obstacle, and assume you are winning. This is your prescription for success unlimited.

PRAYER: "Heavenly Father, my heart is full today with praise and thanksgiving ... but mostly love. Because of love I cast aside my doubt, fear, and inferiority, and in their stead claim Your faith, courage, and confidence. I believe that because of You I am able to stand tall in the world in which I live, confident that I have a workable answer to life through Jesus. In His Name. Amen."

When we sow seeds of doubt,
it brings us a harvest
of more and more needs.
Doubt is as real
in its negative way
as faith is
in its positive way.

18

WHY KILL YOURSELF?

You saw me before I was born and scheduled each day of life before I began to breathe.

Psalm 139:16 TLB

The *Los Angeles Times* stated, "More teenagers than ever before are becoming convinced the only way they can solve their problems is by taking their own lives." It has been stated that suicide has become one of the leading causes of death among teenagers, and it is increasing rapidly. Psychiatrists say there seems to be no apparent reason for this rapid increase.

Some of the reasons given for teenage suicide are: family alienation, peer pressures, drugs, and loneliness. No doubt all of this is true. There are youth who feel no real attachment, who feel no one really cares about them and their problems. Loneliness can be a factor for suicide far beyond our wildest dreams. Stop for a moment and look into the faces of today's youth. Who really sees their struggle for identity? A loss of meaningful relationships could drive a youth to despair. Everybody needs somebody! Even Jesus felt alone on the Cross when He cried, "My God, why have you forsaken me?"

Teenager, you have more reason to be alive and achieving today than at any time in the history of the human race. The world is waiting for your young mind to find a cure for cancer and other related killers. Think of the untold millions of people you could save if you were able to discover the cure for cancer.

Underdeveloped nations are looking for somone to help solve their poverty problem. Countless numbers are dying daily for lack of food, medicine, and care. The world needs you today as it has never needed you before.

The magic of thinking big about your world, your future, and yourself could make all the difference in the world to you personally. Everything in you is made to live. You were created to succeed in some particular area which makes you important to God's plan for the human race. "But how do I find that something?" you ask.

Let me suggest several roads to the magic of escaping futility: (1) Practice adding value to everything in life. Ask what you can do to add value to your home, to your room, to your mind. (2) Practice adding value and importance to people. Make it a habit today not to criticize anything or anybody. See some good in everyone you meet. Look for the best and you will find some value in every person. (3) Add value to yourself. Visualize yourself, not as you are, but as you will be.

The price tag the world puts on you is just about the price tag you put on yourself. Make up your mind to see yourself as a person of worth to your family, to your friends, and to God. Why kill yourself when you are somebody important!

PRAYER: "Lord God, I need Your presence in my life today. You are able for my smallest and my greatest prayer, and deep within me I feel a satisfying trust in Your ability to handle my life. Thank You, Jesus; in You I am not cast down but capable of meeting all life's situations with confidence. In the Name of Jesus. Amen."

*Unbelief is
the reverse form of faith.
Releasing faith
will bring you to the peak
of your abilities
and attract good things to you.
You become
a part of a solution instead of
part of a problem.*

19

HOW DO YOU HANDLE CRITICISM?

In God, I have put my trust, I shall not be afraid. What can man do to me?

Psalm 56:11

Criticism can really hurt—if you let it—or it can be your greatest asset. One thing certain about criticism—it reveals hidden weaknesses and blind spots in our lives. Whether you realize it or not, criticism (if properly understood) could be the very best training for your upcoming leadership. The soft-skinned are bruised by it and the thick-skinned are unmoved by it, but the self-confident are educated by it. Criticism means two things: it is a compliment because of jealousy or a cure coming from brutal honesty. It's up to you to decide which way it goes.

The wise person judges himself daily, before the blow of criticism hits him from behind. You can judge yourself, your attitude, your performance, and do it sincerely. It may save you the embarrassment of others doing it for you.

The fool is the person who refuses to believe that others see him differently from what he sees himself. Watch for the little red flags of criticism. It's a warning to your productivity and personality that says "Improve." Not everyone is blind, you know. The little man who is fighting hard for self-acceptance falls to pieces when criticized. The only way to overcome this reaction is to hear what is being said, but don't let it eclipse your self-respect. Correct your course if you think the remark has merit to it. But continue on your journey! Look upon criticism as someone giving you direction toward your destination. Use it in your journey.

You will learn lessons from those who brace themselves against you or dispute with you. But you will learn no lesson if you take it all personally or feel it was unjust. Even your family's opinions are a great help to sharpen the edge of your life—more so than you could have dreamed possible. All resistance makes for progress. On the other hand, the danger of criticism is that you may take it too seriously and quit. Learn to use it like salt and pepper—add just enough to put zest into life and bring out the flavor of living.

Unjust criticism is often a compliment in disguise. There are times when criticism is used to stop you from achieving. Unsought advice or criticism may at times come from competitors who are hoping you will not succeed in what you're doing. They see success in it and are hoping to block you by criticism. The only person who can decide the honest criticism from the dishonest is you. If you know in your heart you are doing the best thing, then take all remarks with reservation for later examination. Once you have examined the remarks of criticism, fit them into your life properly and keep moving. Remember, no one is 100% correct at all times, so don't let it phase you when a blow of criticism hits. If the criticism comes from your coach, wife, husband, or employer, it is no doubt good for you, for the company, or family.

Mix all criticism into your life well, but don't let it sour you. The important thing is to keep moving. In time it will all work its way out for the best. Handle criticism and you can handle success.

PRAYER: "Heavenly Father, You are the Source from whence my joy comes. Today I base my reaction to every situation on the fact that Christ is an immovable object. No matter how I feel, You are the same. Thanks for being a firm guideline to my life. Love others and fill their need through me. In the Name of Jesus. Amen."

*Since you become
what you picture,
be sure your thoughts
and words express
prosperity and blessing
rather than poverty
and defeat.*

20

ATTITUDE MAKES FOR ALTITUDE

For as [a man] thinks within himself, so he is.

Proverbs 23:7 TLB

The fastest way to gain *altitude* in life is by correct *attitude*. Correct attitude in all areas of life makes for joy or sorrow, success or failure, prosperity or poverty. Right attitude is the most important factor in your life.

The simple truth is, you attract to yourself what you really are. Attitude attracts! The position a man holds is related to his disposition. He does not have a good disposition because of his position; he has the position because of his disposition. Someone said, "Prayer is not the position of the body as much as it is the disposition of the soul."

Therefore, your attitude is a reflection of your true image. The way you dress, the manner of your walk and your talk, all speak loudly concerning the real person.

It is my conviction that attitude even has a smell to it. There is a smell of death and there is a smell of life emanating from you each day. In fact, the New Testament teaches you can bring life or death to others by the fragrance of your disposition.

When you establish a healthy attitude toward yourself—because of self-respect—you will establish the same healthy attitude from others. You will discover, when being rejected by others, that you are basically rejecting yourself. Take the humble but positive attitude that people want to be with you and you sincerely want to be with them. You will soon discover a mutual liking for one another.

You must learn to radiate faith and confidence on the premise that you are successful. Have faith and confidence in your area of responsibility. In your field of learning don't take a back seat to any man, no matter what his field of learning may be. In time you'll discover success breeds success. Others who feel confident will enjoy your company because they'll know you are competent in your field.

Attitude grows as you grow. Seek to be a "pro" in your field—this is the best security for your life and future. You will never enrich yourself without enriching others. This is the secret of having riches. The more qualified you become in your area of interest, the greater interest the world will show in you. Grow in your attitude and aptitude, and you will soon discover altitude has come your way.

Goethe, the outstanding German philosopher, said, "Before you can *do* something you must *become* something."

Your attitude is you. Changing attitudes is not easy; it will take time to kill off the weeds of negativism and doubt toward yourself, your job, and your future. The future is always safe and secure for the person who is improving his attitude and abilities. The obstacles he faces daily give him opportunity to improve his ability in overcoming them. He's learned to face obstacles heroically.

When you start to develop the right attitude, you're on the road to success. Adjust your attitude as needed each hour of each day. The sooner you make the adjustment, the sooner satisfaction will flow into your life. Attitude does make for altitude!

PRAYER: "Heavenly Father, I feel especially thankful today for the effect Your positive message has on my attitude. Within the shadow of the Cross I am confident in my life. In my weakness I am made strong by the power of the Holy Spirit. All things count as gain in my life. Thank You! In Christ's Name. Amen."

Never think or talk lack,
for in so doing
you are decreeing lack,
and lack-thoughts create
a condition of lack.
Stress thoughts of plenty.

21

YOU CAN HAVE ANYTHING YOU REALLY WANT

Listen to me! You can pray for anything, and if you believe, you have it; it's yours!

Mark 11:24 TLB

It was Jesus Christ who said, "All things for which you pray and ask, believe that you have received them, and they shall be granted you." To accomplish this miracle you must never hold a negative thought in your mind about what you have wanted and prayed for. "All things are yours." That's a promise!

For you to have anything you really want, you must develop a sharp, clearly defined goal. You can develop this goal in your mind like developing a film. There will be repeated attempts from a thousand forces to destroy or distort this image, but hold to it until it holds you. What you take will eventually take you. This is true of vocation, habits, ideals, and desires. Many of us do not really know what we want, so we live with a vague sense of emptiness. It is impossible for you to gain if you don't know what you want to gain.

There is a law in the universe which I entitle "The Law of Expectancy." That law is operating in you whether you are aware of it or not. It is an eternal law. Let this law of expectancy develop in your heart. Surround your expectancy with patience, perseverance, and practice. Eventually it will produce results in the very thing you want the most. Likewise, some people expect losses, and they are usually never disappointed.

There is another law like the law of expectancy, and that is "The Law of Prosperity." All you need to do to have anything you want is practice these Laws daily in your life. "Whatsoever things you desire . . . you shall have them"—all of them. You need to keep this before your mind each day. You must also remember that, "Whatsoever things you desire . . ." must be for your good and the benefit of others if you expect it to come to pass.

There are many people who want and desire achievement, but they refuse to pay the price to get it. There are no sharp bargains at the discount store of life. If you expect much you must also put much effort into life. This is effort which seems like fun because what you want is part of life's joys.

Here are three little secrets which I want to give to you. You can have anything you want if you follow these three principles: (1) Pray daily for what you really want. (2) Plan on receiving it. (3) Work your plan every day and commit the full result to God.

There will be times when what you want will look far away and out of reach, but keep walking and working toward it. Each step is progress. If there were no difficulties, there would be no discoveries. It is the irritated oyster which nurtures the pearl. Someone said, "A lot of people are itching for what others have, but they don't want to scratch to get it."

Remember, you can have anything you really want if you want it badly enough. Sow the seed of hope, cultivate it faithfully, and watch it grow to maturity. Hold what you want in the depth of your heart daily, and it will sprout into the fullness of life tomorrow. Now to get what you want, get going today. It's no good sitting around just talking or even thinking; you've got to get going! You can have anything you really want if you want it badly enough!

Desire is the secret of all attainment.

PRAYER: "Precious Lord, by Your Word all things are made possible to me. Today I accept all that You have for me and by faith I lay hold of the promise of God for life and life more abundant. Make my face shine Your love, my mouth speak Your praise, and my heart do Your will to the glory of the Father and the good of those lives I touch. In Christ's Name. Amen."

*Don't build too small;
you may be led into
trying to practice economy
only to find in the long run
it was more costly.*

22

THE MAGIC OF ENTHUSIASM

Whatever your hand finds to do . . . do it with all your might.
Ecclesiastes 9:10 TLB

Let's discover how you can be vital and alive winners by practicing the magic of enthusiasm. Enthusiasm is that priceless quality that makes everything different. Enthusiasm puts color in the voice and a gleam in the eye; it is the winning feeling in a handshake. There is a vibration emanating from the person who has the magic of enthusiasm. Everyone he touches knows he is full of this great and wonderful magic.

The person with enthusiasm lives abundantly *in spite of* and not *because of* his situation. He has learned to live from within instead of from without. He is becoming something other than what he is. An enthusiastic person has as many problems as the next guy. The difference is, his eyes are not on the distasteful, but on the opportunities of living. He refuses to criticize and find fault with life and all its ramifications.

He remembers that success is built in times of pain as well as in times of pleasure. He knows the pearl begins as a pain in the oyster's "stomach." The magic of enthusiasm turns prison cells into choir lofts. It worked for Paul and Silas when they sat in prison and sang praises. The magic of enthusiasm can make a home out of a log cabin, but without it a palace can become a prison.

The magic of enthusiasm can make a routine job glamorous. Its magic touch brings sunshine into the sick room, hope to the despairing, and courage to the disheartened. Turn on the enthusiasm and watch the shadows flee.

There are people reading this who could turn their whole world around if they would turn on enthusiasm. Many of us have lost jobs, promotions, money, and marriages because our lives were dull and colorless. I have met some of the most learned people in the world who lacked enthusiasm, and therefore their knowledge gained them little personal satisfaction. I have talked with leaders whose enthusiastic point of view was dull about the hope of the world and the future of the human race. The vital power of enthusiasm was lacking in their lives; their leadership lacked color and zest.

The vital power of enthusiasm can take a loser and make him a winner.

Being optimistic is a true sign of a winner. A winner is not a blind optimist; he just believes things don't need to remain as they are. He knows there is a possibility of change in everything.

Nobel prize winner Sir Edward V. Appleton, the Scottish physicist, was asked the secret of his amazing discovery. He replied, "It was enthusiasm. I rate enthusiasm even above professional skill."

Without enthusiasm, one would not endure the self-discipline and sacrifice which is so vital in developing a skill for creating possibilities out of impossibilities.

PRAYER: "Heavenly Father, I feel alive in my soul today—alive to the reality of Jesus Christ and the fact that He has changed my life. Fill me anew with the Holy Spirit; make me able to share the positive message of salvation and the abundant life offered through the Person of Jesus Christ. In His Name. Amen."

*Whatever weakens your reason,
or impairs the tenderness
of your conscience,
or obscures your sense of God,
or increases the strength
of your body over your mind,
is wrong.*

23

ASSUME FOR THE MOMENT . . .

And God is able to make all grace abound to you, that always having all sufficiency in everything, you may have an abundance for every good deed.

II Corinthians 9:8 TLB

I want you to assume for a moment that you have everything you want. Why? Until you assume or act as if you have what you want, you probably will never get it. Act as if you believe; bet your life on the very thing you're believing for.

The very fear of failure insures failure!

Fear is the great destroyer of all creativity.

Act in faith, and assume you are successful! Positive action brings the assurance of your success. Begin by assuming that God is no respecter of persons. Assume for the moment you have tremendous capacities and abilities to do what you have always wanted to do. Act as if you believe it!

I think St. Peter could have walked on the water all day if he hadn't begun to assume he was sinking. He was actually acting his way to a miracle. When he stopped assuming that he could walk on the water, he sank! Moments before, he had been on the water, but now the water was on him. Jesus said that after you pray, start acting as though what you prayed for is now reality and you will receive what you want. There is no magic in this; it's a universal law.

You will become what you pretend to be. The actor on stage must not only know his part, he must become the part. It's not hard to tell the difference between *acting* a part and *being* a part. The sooner you *become* the part, the sooner you will feel the satisfaction, security, and success of that part.

Many of us refuse to act the part lest we deceive ourselves. Actually it is really the other way around. You need to *un*-deceive yourself. You have been brainwashed too long. You need to convince yourself that you are able to be the person you've always wanted to be. You actually accept yourself as a failure quicker than you accept yourself as a success.

Assume for the moment that you are where you want to be. Hold that before your mind each day. You may have to readjust the image of it daily and hourly. Life has ways of knocking your lens out of focus. Keep adjusting your lens as often as necessary by study and association with like-minded people. Don't permit prejudice or false egotism to keep you from doing this.

Let me make this clear. For you to assume that you are or have what you want is by no means a call to laziness or dishonesty. It's just the opposite. If you assume to be a writer then you must proceed to write. If, on the other hand, you assume that you are an actor, then seek the stage. Someone said, "All growth depends on activity."

To assume does not mean to be idle; it means to be in motion. Whatever steps are necessary to reach the actuality of your dreams, you must take those steps, starting today. The very fact that you are moving toward your goal by assuming is the secret of your motivation and achievement. It is the image of having arrived which spurs you on to achievement.

There are three simple steps to the realization of your dreams. (1) Assume for the moment you are what you want to be. (2) Act like you would if you had everything you want. (3) Keep on acting out the part until you achieve it.

Assuming each moment is the key to getting what you want.

PRAYER: "Heavenly Father, I recognize Your sufficiency today; You are all things to my life. You are my salvation, my daily living, and my very future, and I desire Your plan for my life. I act in faith. I take all I need by faith. It is mine today. In the Name of Jesus. Amen."

Prayer without work
is perversion.
Work without prayer
is presumption.

24

SEEK FOR GREATNESS OF HEART

For God sees not as man sees, for man looks at the outward appearance, but the Lord looks at the heart.

1 Samuel 16:7 TLB

Louis Untermeyer says, "Greatness has always been a mark to aim at. It is not only inspiring but imperative to think continually of those who were truly great. Soldiers on forgotten fields of battle, scientists in makeshift laboratories, stubborn idealists fighting to save a lost cause, teachers who would not be intimidated, tireless doctors and faithful preachers—the anonymous army of dreamers and doers—all of these by their very living fought for everyone. They sacrificed hours of ease for our comfort; they gave up safety for our security. Glorifying the heroic spirit of man, they added to our stature."

Seek the company of the great in heart, for there is where greatness is found. The most profound are the most humble. Xenophanes said, "It takes a wise man to recognize a wise man." Fools only recognize fools. "Deep calls unto deep," the Bible says. The depth and greatness of two people can cross all barriers, creeds, and political views. Why? Because greatness responds to greatness, no matter what the situation may be. Greatness belongs to the universe, like air to the lungs. All may breathe freely of it, irrespective of nation, religion, color, or position in life.

The great in heart cannot be forced to conformity.

He that is great in heart refuses to be restricted by man-made forms. He belongs to the universe, and while he is free to *do* he is also free to *become*.

Keep company with fools and you'll become one. Seek out the company of the great, but do not hope to ride on their coat-tails to greatness. For you to find greatness it must be developed within as well as sought from without. But do not despair, for in due season all will begin to take notice that there is the sound of greatness in you. The world will beat a path to your door to hear your words, feel your spirit, or only to look upon the beauty which greatness has molded into you.

It was not the spirit of an egotist who said "Look on us." (Acts 3:4 KJV) The first man to say this was St. Peter, one of the truly greats. You actually take on the air or atmosphere or stature of what you look at the most and love. Is it any wonder that true greatness draws success to itself like the rose draws sunshine? A man is known by the company he keeps and seeks.

Self-identification may be found by association. But for you to stay in the association of the great, you must be aiming for greatness of heart continually. It must become your mark, your goal. You must press toward it daily, or the outcome of your association with greatness will be rejection—rejection by those whom you admire, because they felt the insincerity of your aspiration and association. This rejection could send you back to the end of the line, to the end of life's promotion. You must know yourself, trust yourself, and be yourself—your very best self!

Seek for greatness of heart! The great will be glad to have you in their company.

PRAYER: "Father, my heart sings with praise as I consider the greatness of Your work among us. I now release faith, thereby drawing to myself the miracle of renewed life through the power of the spoken Word. Anoint my mind, enlarge my concept, and motivate my life to excellence. In Christ's Name. Amen."

Faith lifts up its hand
through the threatening clouds,
lays hold of Him
who has all power
in heaven and earth.
Faith makes the uplook good,
the outlook bright,
the inlook favorable,
and the future glorious.

25

AFFECTION ATTRACTS

Love each other with brotherly affection and take delight in honoring each other.

Romans 12:10 TLB

C. S. Lewis said, "The humblest of all love is affection." Affection is modest; it has in it a feeling of privacy. In some sense of the word, affection is unlimited, reaching out to everyone and everything at all times. Nature calls forth affection from each of us. A tender touch can awaken affection. The only safety for this unlimited affection is intelligent direction. The need for affection and the need to give affection is basic in all human personality. The danger comes when affection is not controlled. You cannot deny the need for affection. You can only direct it.

We greatly desire the affection of other people. Even an animal desires affection. This is normal. But extreme demands for affection can scare others away from us because they sense it is an unhealthy attachment. When we are overly ambitious with our affections we usually seal up the very fountain from which we wish to drink. C. S. Lewis goes on to say, "True affection, because it is free from all wish to ruin, humiliate, or domineer, can say with good grace what would be, without affection, arrogant and spiteful and ruthless." Affection attracts!

The overly affectionate can become perverted, as the mother who makes her family miserable because she "lives for them." The truly affectionate mother does not wish to dominate the child or the family to prove she loves them. She learns to live and let live under the care of her affection.

There is the professor who teaches the student to become a scholar, only to find himself jealous of the student's success. His affection becomes perverted when the student succeeds. This is a loss of true affection from the professor to the student. He should be happy that the student is gaining in knowledge. Affection shares the glory with another.

Affection between husband and wife can be a honeymoon or a hell. The Bible says, "Husbands, love your wives." Affection is a spiritual and a biological need. The wife is to show her affection by responding to the God-like love of her husband.

Being in love is not primarily sexual. Sex is a part of love but surely not the whole of love. The concept you hold of affection, or of being in love, will have a direct bearing on your success and personal satisfaction. Affection is attractive, but be careful you attract the right person. Of all the emotions in the human body, none seems as right as affection. It can at times feel divine. That's what makes it dangerous.

If the love-desire, the feeling of affection, is allowed to have its way unconditionally, it can become a demon. But set affection in a proper relationship between husband and wife or between friends of mutual respect and interest, and you have found the nearest thing to grace.

Develop the affectionate side of your nature, but teach it the laws of right conduct. The affectionate heart will attract friends, business, wealth, and prosperity but at the same time danger. When affection attracts let it be governed by honesty and good judgment. Affection can be your greatest asset or biggest liability. It's up to you how you handle the growing heart of affection. You cannot deny the need for affection. It must be fed, led, and directed in order to bring out the sparkle of life.

PRAYER: "Heavenly Father, I stand before you as a child, reaching toward You for affection and Your gentle hand of love upon my head. You have touched my life in a real and vital way and I pledge my redeemed life to Your Service. Flow through me to touch others with the same love I have needed and found so real through Jesus Christ. Amen."

Faith is dead to doubts,
dumb to discouragement,
blind to impossibilities,
knows
nothing but success.

26

POLITENESS IS PROFITABLE

Let us not lose heart in doing good, for in time we shall reap if we do not grow weary.

Galations 6:9 TLB

Confucius said, "Behave towards everyone as if receiving a great guest." The polite person has an atmosphere of affability. He is easy to speak to and is courteous and amiable in response to others' wishes. He is sociable; he has a graciousness about his whole person. In the words of St. Paul, "Let your moderation be known unto all men," or let your gentleness be known to all men. This is the polite person who is finding profit by living this way. The affable person is down-to-earth, easy to approach. He has the human-saint image, but he is not among the untouchables.

This trait of character needs to be developed in all people who are seeking to be successful. Every student needs to develop affability; it is a most important factor for teachers and people in sales or leadership. Profit, gain, and recognition are summed up in politeness and affability. They are indispensable if you want to be a winner. When you practice affability, you are practicing one of the greatest virtues in the world.

The failure withdraws from people and is unsocial. His inferior mind holds him back from social communication and contact. The "stiff shirt" is usually unresponsive and very insecure.

The world of success will not ask to see your degrees, only the temperature of your soul.

Jesus Christ was never so holy as to be impolite. He had a sense of being down-to-earth with humanity and was interested in meeting their needs. The most outstanding homes, companies, and institutions in the world are those who practice the art of affability.

The winning life is one which responds to living. It has the ability to see the need and feel the desires in others and seeks to respond graciously to that need or desire. The greatest sin we commit against each other is our cold indifference. You don't need to shoot a man to kill him; just ignore him and he will die of love malnutrition.

You remember the expression, "Honey attracts—vinegar distracts." The sweetness of disposition attracts outstanding positions. Very few people hold leadership for long unless the attitudes of affability and amiability are being manifested. We attract to us what we are.

I want you to see other people as you see yourself. Look upon them as needing self-respect, recognition, and security. Everyone, no matter what his bank balance may be, wants to feel accepted, loved, and understood. In many respects all men are brothers—human brothers. There are people who seem to think they don't need others to survive. Only an idiot would practice living in that disillusioned state.

Any good achievement is success, but permanent success can be predicted for the person by his response to his first taste of success. If he remains touchable, human, and open for communication, it can be predicted that he will enjoy lasting success. Politeness is profitable. Learn the art of affability, amiability, and being easily approached. The untouchables are not usually the winners in the struggles of life.

PRAYER: "Precious Lord, I bow my heart in reverence before Your throne and acknowledge the Son, Jesus Christ, as Saviour of my soul, giving Him honor and recognition for the work of perfection He is doing in my life. Make me sensitive to the bidding of the Holy Spirit, that my life might touch others and count for gain in Your Kingdom here on earth. In the Name of Christ. Amen"

The blessing of the Lord
sweeps away
all that would impede its course.
Nothing can stand before it.
Constantly expect God's miracles.
Don't expect results
in keeping with your capacity.
The human family
is the only channel
from which you can
receive your living
while giving service.

27

PEOPLE SEE YOU FIRST—THEN YOUR ACCOMPLISHMENTS

And we know that God causes all things to work together for good to those who love God, to those who are called according to His purpose.

Romans 8:28 TLB

An institution may spread itself over the entire world and may employ a hundred thousand men, but the average person usually forms his judgment of it through his contact with one individual. If that person is rude or inefficient, it will take a lot of kindness and efficiency to overcome that first impression. Every member of an organization who comes in contact with the public is a salesman, and the impression he makes is an advertisement—good or bad.

Your whole future depends upon what you *are* (disposition and attitude) as much as what you *do*. I would rather sacrifice the talented person who has a bad attitude than to have progress with the possibility of a "blowout" down the road with a negative-minded individual. All the good he may do has built into it the possibility of an explosion if he is unable to control his disposition.

People will look beyond your accomplishments to see you. They see you first, then your work.

"Behind all success is truth, and truth has its own reward," said Dr. Albert Schweitzer.

Sandy Duncan proves that success follows truth when she

says, "I feel that everything that happens, happens for the best. Take the loss of my sight in one eye. Without that happening I would never have met Tom, the doctor whom I have just married. My whole attitude toward life has changed. My career is still important, but it isn't everything in my life anymore. Everything seems to be put in a more proper perspective now. Until this happened, life was too easy. Now I've learned to live with the fact that it can have its ups and downs—and I appreciate the ups much more." Sandy Duncan found the secret of being greater than her accomplishments. First you see the girl, then her performance.

The actor is always greater than his acts—or at least he should be. As one old man in the South put it, "What you are speaks so loud I can't hear what you say." The eyes see more than the ears hear.

Truly successful people know the foundation must be solid if the superstructure is to be strong. The Bible says, "If the foundations be destroyed, what can the righteous do?" Your accomplishments will outlast you if they are built on truth. Seek to do something that will outlive your life.

Impressions are not usually forgotten, especially the first impression.

People are the best advertisements of any institution. Let it become your project that people see you first when they're thinking of the institution you represent. Jesus said, "You are my witnesses." He also said, "You are the light of the world." People see you, then your accomplishments. Keep in mind that your future depends upon what you are, in disposition and attitude, as well as on what you do.

PRAYER: "Lord God, You know my mind today and You know my need better than I know myself. I feel alert to the Holy Spirit and I willingly open my heart to Him. I'll do Your bidding, just direct my way. Manifest Yourself to me, fill me completely. I appropriate Your peace and Your joy for my own life. Be so real that I might be able to introduce You into every situation with effortless energy. In Christ's Name. Amen."

We definitely hope
we shall be preserved
from mistakes
and careless words and acts
but we shall find that
with God's blessing upon us
even our serious blunders
do not ultimately hinder
His purpose.
When He blesses the work
nothing can wreck it,
for the transforming power
of His blessing
turns liabilities
into enriching assets.

28

SIMPLICITY LOOKS PROFOUND

Watch over your heart with all diligence, for from it flow the springs of life.

Proverbs 4:23 TLB

All great truths are simple; they are only profound to the doubter. The humble in heart accept simplicity and thereby make it seem profound. Simplicity reduces truth, life, and experience to its lowest minimum, but at the same time lifts truth and life to its greatest maximum.

Stupidity is not simplicity, and simplicity is not ignorance.

Simplicity is a matter of the heart. It is in the spirit of man. It is the survival of the best in life. Simplicity cuts the weeds of waste and the underbrush of loss and focuses instead on the seed and its potential. It has a way of looking through life. Simplicity is tuned to the voice of the universe. It hears sounds which make sense, while others only hear noises. When St. Paul was converted on the road to Damascus, he heard a voice, while others standing around said, "It thundered." The sound made one man a saint but only caused others to wonder!

What you hear, see, and feel in the universe depends on the development of your simplicity. It is like two men looking into the Grand Canyon. One said, when seeing the depth of the world-famous canyon, "This is the hand of God. I am amazed." The other man looked over the edge and spit. He said, "That's the first time I ever spit a mile."

The index to your simplicity is your reaction to the wonders of life! Many of us walk by the secrets of the world and hardly recognize them. We are caught up with gnats, flies, and noise. Simplicity can look at an apple, enjoy a raindrop, feel the wind, and find joy. It does not need a circus to entertain it. The one who seeks simplicity walks in the night with his thoughts, has a prayer for his dreams, seeks victories, enjoys companionship, loves the face of a child. All of these bring joy to the heart of the simple. It is joy unspeakable and full of glory. This is the reward of developing simplicity.

But no character can be simple unless it is based on truth. It must live in harmony with its conscience and ideals. It is what one psychologist calls "Reality Therapy." It is living within your own heart. "Out of the heart flows the issues of life," we are told.

Simplicity is destroyed by any attempt to live in harmony with public opinion. Public opinion is a syndicate. You must live by the standards, ideals, and goals of your life as *you* see them. This is not a call for rebellion, it is not an urge for riots. It is a call for truth, honesty, and personal pride.

Simplicity is a restful soul. It has a contempt for the nonessentials.

Simplicity is not paralyzed or awestruck by the overpowering. It has no inferiority, paralysis, or superiority plagues.

The restlessness in our society causes war and heartache. People who carry the destiny of great enterprises are usually quiet in heart, modest in talk, and unassuming in manner. The secret of all greatness is simplicity. It is reducing tons of ore to nuggets of gold.

PRAYER: "Almighty God, Creator and Saviour, I stand before You today with love in my heart, conscious that I need to have You in total control of every area of my life. My primary goal for this day is to be aware of the power of Jesus Christ working in and through me. In His Name. Amen."

*In "fighting
against circumstances"
a man is continually
revolting against
an effect without,
while all the time
nourishing
its cause in his heart.*

29

YOUR UNREALIZED POSSIBILITIES

Now to Him who is able to do exceeding abundantly beyond all that we ask or think according to the power that works within us.

Ephesians 3:20 TLB

If you could see the unrealized potential within your mind, you would be amazed. The greater part of you is unseen. It is a known fact that 9/10 of an iceberg is below water. Could it be that 9/10 of your ability, possibility, and brain power are out of sight?

It was William Jordon who said, "No man could face the radiant revelation of the latent powers and forces within him, underlying the weak, narrow life he is living. He would fall behind, blinded and prostrate, as did Moses before the burning bush."

The greatest moment of your life is when you see yourself as you are! You were made with a reserve power of energy, motivation, creativity, and health. The forces of nature within you really come to the top when called upon to do so.

All of nature responds to need. We are concerned about pollution, and we must be, but if man fails to clean up the mess, nature will eventually do it, even if she must destroy the human race to do so. We had better work with the cleaning power of Mother Nature, for she can be stern!

It takes only a little effort and a few minutes a day to clear away the rubbish in your mind, to discover unused powers waiting to be put into circulation. You are built like a great pipe organ—all ready, but needing someone who will pull out the stops, push the pedals, and organize the sound. Life can be a symphony or it can be chaos!

Your mind only releases the potential when it is absolutely necessary. The garden of the gods has a strong tendency to become the jungle of demons, if left to itself.

Devils are created when the good is left unused. Evil is nothing more than good gone bad. You must remember that demons were at one time angels.

The potential of nature is seen when animals change color to adjust to the season of their environment. New environment calls for new harmony. Proper conditions start the recreative powers of nature to meet new demands. If this is true in nature, how much more is it true of you. You were made to succeed, to grow, to develop, and conquer your world. It is as if God says to man, "Take charge!" If you fail to take command of your situation, your situation will take command of you.

What you fail to control will eventually control you. Life is teaching you how to survive.

At some point in your life, the sooner the better, something will happen—a crisis, a death, an opportunity, which will be the grand opening of your unused resources. If you fail to tap the resources at that moment, it could mean loss to you.

If you are wise you will welcome the abrupt blow and use it to unlock the potential that has been there in you and gone unrealized. Put forth the effort—you'll be amazed at the potential ability which was in you all the while.

You may fail in a dozen different lines of activity and then succeed brilliantly in a phase in which you were unconscious of any ability. You are a winner when you dare more today than you did yesterday. You have yet to discover your unrealized possibilities!

PRAYER: "Heavenly Father, I recognize You as Creator, Saviour, and Master of my life. I ask Your forgiveness for the times I've failed you. Thank You for not binding me to failure, but understanding, forgiving, and even using it to build Your Kingdom. Now make my life desirable to others; give me opportunities to share the Life of Christ with those around me. In His Name. Amen."

The soul attracts
that which it secretly harbors
and that which it loves,
and also
that which it fears;
it reaches the height
of its cherished aspirations,
it falls to the level
of its unchastened desires—
and circumstances
are the means by which
the soul receives its own.

30

LET'S BOIL OVER

I know you well—you are neither hot nor cold; I wish you were one or the other! But since you are merely lukewarm, I will spit you out of my mouth!

Revelation 3:15, 16 TLB

It was Walt Whitman who said, "I was simmering, really simmering, until Emerson brought me to a boil." As a result, Whitman produced poetry which is immortal. Many of us are simmering, not yet at the boiling point. The cooking process never starts until you pass the simmering temperature and reach the boiling point.

Once you go beyond simmering to boiling, you will discover talents, powers, and abilities you never dreamed were yours. Whatever causes you to boil, bringing you to a heat of enthusiasm, is a blessing. The spiritual ear of your heart can turn off the elements of failure, defeat, and despondency. The unsuspected powerhouse in you will only be discovered from the boiling furnace of faith and a deep-seated desire to achieve. Charles M. Schwab said, "A man can succeed at almost anything for which he has unlimited enthusiasm."

The cold and damp-spirited create little and cause much loss. They are in the crowd saying, "It can't be done." If someone fails, they are eager to announce, "I told you so." Seldom do these people win a Nobel Prize or bring about a new creation for the betterment of mankind.

Let's boil over! There are countless numbers of people who could help change their world if they would only come to a boil. There are many homes on dead-heat. No life, warmth, or love is being activated in the family.

Think of the churches which are like cold storages instead of hot furnaces. I read where a church caught fire one night and the whole town came out to watch it burn. Someone in the crowd remarked, "I've never seen so many people at the church." A bystander replied, "That's the first time the church has been on fire."

Fire attracts!

But I want you to understand that enthusiasm, or boiling over, is regulated fire in a special way. It is fire under control, the only kind that counts. Fire must be harnessed. Wild fire only destroys.

The world is yours when your fire is hot, directed, and regulated. To boil over is not the same as being out of control. It is a guided, directed fire, producing the desired result. Another said it this way: "Triumph is *umph* added to *try*!" That's boiling over.

You can come to a boil today. How? Let me give you 6 short but meaningful directions: (1) Do more than exist—live. (2) Do more than look—see. (3) Do more than read—absorb. (4) Do more than hear—listen. (5) Do more than think—ponder. (6) Do more than talk—act. Put these six fuels in your life and you will come to a boil.

There are, of course, people who are in the "I could care less" category. They are neither hot nor cold. They live in a kind of sickly neutrality. You can't say they are either hot or cold. The Bible refers to these people as "lukewarm," and God said, "I will spue them out of my mouth." That's rough treatment, but that's the way life and God handle the lukewarm.

Start today to put heat in your heart. Turn on the fuel, put on the coal, get excited about an idea, a project, or something you are doing. Help change the world—your world. Push the temperature from simmering to boiling. There are unlimited resources in you if you will come to a boil.

PRAYER: "Heavenly Father, my heart is full of love and praise for You today. You have given me a vision of myself which I can become through the power of the Holy Spirit: happy, fulfilled, and useful. I accept the challenge of a changing life with excitement. Train me to be a useful tool in Your hands. In the Name of Jesus. Amen."

*Every miracle
has the fingerprint
of man on it.*

31

CHARACTER IS COLLATERAL

He has granted to us His precious and magnificent promises, in order that by them you might become partakers of the divine nature.

II Peter 1:4

The single best collateral in your life is your character. As long as you are building character you are investing in your future. The deepest form of poverty is a lack of character. Let a man lose everything in life except his character and he still has the winning edge. Character is the foundation of all superstructures. "As [a man] thinks within himself, so he is" (Proverbs 23:7).

The man of character has with him at all times his savings, bonds, securities, and his universe. He is the performer; he is the act, the show, and the productive plant all in one. He has the ability to be what he wants to be at any given time. Building character is like building a bridge over troubled waters. All men may forsake you, but you never forsake yourself when building true character.

The man of character soon discovers he is many men in one. Various images have their habitations in his soul. He is a musician, a painter, a poet, a prophet—seeking to set his life to tone, color, words, and convictions. Building character is like forming a team or assembling an orchestra. It is like storing facts in the brain or money in the bank. The amazing thing about the collateral of character is that you have the key to unlock it whenever needed. No other person has the key to your storage vault but you. This adds importance and dignity to your life.

It is refreshing to know you have a supply of good character when the pressure is on. Belief in yourself, your abilities, and your hunches adds color and zest to your inner life.

Reputation is what others think of you. Character is what you are. Many of us spend most of our time being concerned with what others think of us and neglect the important matter—what we are able to think of ourselves. This is not saying we always *like* what we are, but the important fact to remember is that we are always improving. It would be a tragedy if you liked everything about yourself all the time. The ability to build character is the ability to see where the need for improvement lies and there focus your attention. Don't despair when you find weaknesses. Say as St. Paul did, "When I am weak, then am I strong."

The value you put on yourself is usually the value others put on you. If your true value has not been recognized yet, don't faint—there will come a time when your "showing" will be ready. Most men are never a public success until they're a private success.

Keep building the collateral of character even though you're unknown. There will come a time when the world will say, "Where has he been all these years?" Only you will be able to answer that question, for you will remember the long years spent building the collateral of character. The time will come when the collateral will pay off. The single best investment in your future is the character you're building.

How do you build character? Here are some guidelines: (1) Be true to yourself. (2) Finish the job you're doing, no matter how small. (3) Speak well of your enemies. (4) Pray for guidance in your daily work. (5) Read something great every day. These things will help you build a stronger character, thereby assuring you of success.

111

PRAYER: "Lord God, I come before You with a thankful heart today, thankful that I am not the person I was yesterday and eager for the person I will be tomorrow. For the most important day of my life, today, help me to live in positive reaction to the power of the Holy Spirit within me. In the Name of Jesus. Amen."

When anxiety begins, faith ends.

32

CHEER UP!

In me you may have peace. In the world you have tribulation, but take courage; I have overcome the world.
                                                    John 16:33 TLB

It was Ralph Waldo Emerson who said, "There is a solution for every problem, and the soul's highest duty is to be of good cheer." If a problem can be stated, it can be solved! To say, "Cheer up," is not to ignore a problem or bypass a situation; good cheer is the first step toward solving all problems. Jesus shouted to the disciples, "Be of good cheer; it is I; be not afraid." This was said to the disciples when they were in a sinking ship in the midst of a devastating storm. It is amazing what can happen when a little cheer is shown.

The other day my wife and I went out for breakfast. We went into a beautiful little restaurant and were seated. The waitress came with two glasses of water and menus, and her hands were full. I expected to hear the familiar greeting, "How are you and may I help you?" As I helped take the water and free her hands, she said with enthusiasm to my wife, "I bet he's nice to have around." That did it! I felt ten years younger and immediately our spirits lifted because of her cheerfulness. What a radiant person she was. The doors of communication were opened and everyone cheered up!

Cheerfulness is one of the great virtues of success. It's like putting fuel on the fire. With it you can conquer gloom, dispel darkness, and heal the mind of loneliness. If I had to make a choice between a talented person and a cheerful person of lesser talent, I would take the cheerful person.

The amazing results which come from cheerfulness are almost unlimited. The tendency of the human heart is toward gloom, but sunny personalities can be developed as well as inherited.

Most of the world needs cheering up. Our college campuses remind me, at times, of a penal institution. Professors have forgotten that students learn faster and better in the atmosphere of cheer. Our shops, offices, and campuses not only need production, but cheerful production. Happy people put out more work than unhappy people do. Show me someone who is cheerful and I'll show you someone who has unlimited possibilities.

Let me suggest several ways for you to learn to be cheerful: (1) Find the reasons in your life at this moment to be of good cheer. It can't be all bad. Make a list right now of the things you consider to be helpful and for which you are grateful. (2) Try to remember the worst thing that has ever happened to you. You lived through that; ask yourself how. Find the answer and you have another stone on which to step. (3) Think of one person you know that is glad you're alive. Everybody has somebody. (4) Go to the Bible and read the Psalms. There are 36 "fear nots" in the Bible, one for each day. Find the one you need! Above everything else, remember that you are made in the image of God. He loves you! Learn these lessons of cheer and watch the lights of your soul turn on every day for the rest of your life. Cheer up! Be glad you're alive!

PRAYER: "Heavenly Father, I am aware of Your greatness, of Your wonderful love, and of the control You have on my world. I put my trust in you. I give all that I have, secure in the knowledge that You are able to do far above all I could ever hope for in my life. I let go of my reserve, leaving You free to work within me. Do it now, in the Name of Jesus. Amen."

*True prayer is joined
to the
Spirit of the universe.*

33

LET'S ENJOY THIS MOMENT

My chosen ones shall wear out the work of their hands . . .
for they are the offspring of those blessed by the Lord, and
their descendants with them.

Isaiah 65:22, 23 TLB

Everyone reading these lines wants to be happy. The whole world needs happiness! Don't be chagrined or feel guilty about that desire, it's as natural as breathing. The unending journey of the human heart is to find peace and happiness. Happiness could be health to the mind or wealth to the person. The effects of true happiness are almost without number. The mind works smoothly and effectively when the heart is contented. "Contentment is great gain," the Bible tells us. If one has found contentment, it's amazing how wealthy and happy he feels.

The amount of work a person can produce, when the mind is tranquil, is unlimited. Tranquility brings triumph to the life. The Roman emperor Cicero said, "The happy life lies in tranquility of mind." How true!

It is my conviction that positive-minded people are happy in spite of their circumstances and not because of them. If you could see inside the hearts and minds of great men who found achievement, you would discover that their minds were like a pools of water—quiet and deep. The secret of being happy is to find happiness within yourself. Beware of looking for it outside yourself. True motivation must spring from within the depths of the person. "From [the heart] flow the springs of life," we are told in Proverbs 4:23.

There will be countless distractions which will seek to disturb your inner mind from being happy. You must learn the secret of shutting out those disturbing thoughts. Develop the habit of drawing from the deep well inside you. There you will find a steady stream of contentment and joy.

Happiness is a deep contentment of the soul. One who is happy cannot be permanently ruined. Let me reemphasize that happiness is the goal of every normal human being. God wants you to be happy. All of life wants you to be happy. It's up to you to make it so.

There are people who have given up in life. They feel true happiness is not to be found in this world, that there is no infallible formula for happiness. They feel each day is only another day on the treadmill of living; loneliness haunts their every move, their pessimistic conviction says happiness is unattainable.

But there is a pure happiness which is a result of your own decision, discovery, and destination. You are the builder of your own world. The world within is the product of your design. Joy does not depend on outward circumstances. When our sense of well-being depends on the things around us, we are in trouble.

It has been observed if you pursue happiness, it evades you. Many pursue it in the yesterday, always looking back; others pursue it in the future, always looking forward; others pursue it in the present, and it escapes them.

Let me suggest 5 simple steps to enjoy this moment and find happiness. (1) Be grateful for life as it is. (2) Seek to improve your life by every means possible. (3) Think of achieving something worthwhile for you and your loved ones today. (4) Plunge into an active life. Don't sit on the bench; move out where the action is. (5) Live one day at a time. Enjoy this moment now and tomorrow will hold even more happiness for you.

You can only live this instant. That's all you'll ever live. We feel we are unhappy because of the trouble we have had or always will have. Free yourself from yesterday and tomorrow. Use this moment, this instant, to the very fullest. The happier a man is, the more things he is able to accomplish and enjoy.

PRAYER: "Lord God, You are the same yesterday, today, and forever. Thanks for being an unchanging rock on which I can base my life. I put my trust in the Person of Jesus and dedicate myself to spread the Word of His love. Change my desires until I always react in a natural and positive way, leaving You free to do a great work in and through my life. Amen."

*We must bet our very lives
on the validity
of a Scriptural principle
to win in
the battles of life.*

34

THE MOST POPULAR FORM OF SUICIDE IS WORRY

Let him have all your worries and cares, for he is always thinking about you and watching everything that concerns you.
                                                    I Peter 5:7 TLB

Worry is the most respectable form of killing yourself. It is a slow disease of the mind which cuts the nerve to motivation. The bright, creative power of the imagination is paralyzed by the polio of worry; the young are made old by it and the old are soon sent to the grave because of it. Homes become death cells because of worry. College campuses have turned from readin', 'riting, and 'rithmetic to riots, rebellion, and retaliation because of worry. It kills the appetite, causes insomnia, spoils the taste for living, irritates the disposition, warps the personality, weakens the mind, and saps our energy. Worry is soul poison.

Tension builds high in the life plagued by worry. Conflict between husband and wife increases because of worry. Worry takes the place of prayer, planning, and practical pleasure of living. Someone said jokingly, "Why pray, when you can worry." We must learn to cut off the worry habit or the worry habit will cut us off. We must decide which force will be the stronger and therefore control our lives—the force of worry or the force of peace.

Worry eats like a worm on the marrow of the bones. Grief, fear, or sorrow can obscure the eye from the beauty and excitement of today. When the inner voice, that "still, small voice," is weakened because of the overwhelming voice of worry, there is great danger of your potential becoming limited.

Worry is forethought gone to seed.

Worry is discounting the possibility of change. It is the mother of many illegitimate children, like deceit, despondency, defeat, and death itself. Worry draws the mind away from duty. It saps the mind of its creative powers. Students who worry usually make low grades; teachers who worry produce neurotic students; management that worries triggers strikes and unrest among labor; the production line is cut down because the laboring man is worried. Because of worry, preachers produce damp souls in their congregations, lovers have separated, and wars have ripped the world apart. It is the number one enemy of mankind. It is your personal barrier to success and achievement.

Here are a few guidelines to stop the worry habit: (1) Put more effort today in what you're doing; it means less worry tomorrow. (2) Plan the very best you can now and don't panic if your plans fail. There are more roads than one to your destination. It's the destination that counts, not the detours. (3) Act each day as if you have no permanent concerns. The Bible tells you, "Be anxious for nothing." Remember, nothing is permanent in this world. (4) Do a little each day toward improving your future, but don't make the mistake of living in the tomorrow. Build this moment. It's amazing how the provisions for tomorrow take care of themselves. (5) Rehearse your duty in your mind before you face your public work. See yourself performing in the best possible manner. This helps to kill off the worry of failure. See yourself not as worried, fretting, and failing, but rehearse yourself daily in your mind as a successful individual. Practice these five suggestions each day and you will kill the worry habit before it kills you. You must desire peace, or worry will control you!

PRAYER: "Heavenly Father, I see You today as a God of miracle, able for my situation. I confess I need You in my life. I am willing to open that secret inner chamber of my mind to the positive influence of Jesus Christ. Thank You that I may excel in You. In Christ's Name. Amen."

I am afraid of nothing.
What can death do to me?
I've already died.
I've come back
from my own funeral
and am alive
in the ALIVE.

35

LET'S BREAK THE WORRY RESPONSE

Trust in the Lord with all your heart, and do not lean on your own understanding.

Proverbs 3:5 TLB

It is difficult to worry when you force yourself to do tough thinking and enthusiastic planning. You can create the very situation which occupies your mind. The mind creates. Your worry response is a created habit. It seems the self-preservation urge gets the upper hold on the mind when too much attention is given to it. This becomes a worry-response.

Being occupied, doing the helpful things of life, forces worry thoughts out of life. As animals are taught to respond to certain stimuli, so we may train our minds to respond to certain stimuli. Responses are learned.

Your mind can hold only one thought at a time. If you hold negative, troubled thoughts, you will produce negative and troubled responses in life. Job, one of the Old Testament prophets, said, "The thing I feared has come upon me." He got exactly what he expected. It would be shocking to discover someday that life allowed our minds to govern our providence. On whom would you blame life's situations if that were true?

All habits are acquired. Bad habits are acquired more slowly than good habits. It is never the first or second act which binds us. Evil habits form slowly around the soul and mind, and this is the reason they are so difficult to break. On the other hand, good, sound habits must be grasped quickly and firmly if they are to be acquired.

It seems that good habits evade us; riches and honor are also elusive at times. Evil seems to be near anytime we call for it. Worry, anxiety, and fear are next door to the soul, always ready to enter. Actually, faith, hope, and a positive attitude are eager to establish themselves in our lives, but we must make the choice which of these two forces will control our lives.

Worry is most apt to run you ragged, not when you're in action, but when you are unproductive. King David went to bed with Bathsheba when kings were supposed to be in battle. He chose the bed instead of the battle and had the stinging sword in his household all the days of his life.

If your worry comes from guilt, face it and have it erased. Worry and guilt feelings cut down on productivity and prosperity. Riches and honor could be yours sooner than you think if you would break the worry response. How?

Put yourself in productive action and you're on the first step of the ladder to success. When you can't handle events, let them handle themselves. Someone said, "When we stop fighting the inevitable and unavoidable, we release energy, which enables us to create a richer life." As you break the worry habit, you will find a release of creativity for living.

PRAYER: "Heavenly Father, thank You for changing my life. Thank You for seeing me, not as I was, but as I could become. Thank You for the patience and loving concern that continually challenge me to a life of purpose through Jesus Christ. In His Name. Amen."

*Give yourself up
morning by morning
to be led
by the Holy Spirit
and go forward
praising and at peace,
leaving Him to manage your day.
Count upon His blessing
as a fact
altogether apart from feeling.*

36

WHAT CHRIST MEANS TO ME

God was in Christ reconciling the world to Himself . . .
Therefore, we are ambassadors for Christ . . .
II Corinthians 5:19, 20 TLB

If this message should come to one who is dissatisfied with life, who feels that his own human strength is insufficient for the problems and the tasks of these strenuous times, who is looking for some lift and courage outside his own being, I hope he will frankly face and enthusiastically accept the power which has been found sufficient.

"God was in Christ, reconciling the world to Himself."

Christ means reconciliation; the peace treaty has been signed by His blood. The fear and estrangement that came with sin, the desire to fight against God (growing out of my own sinfulness) has been removed by the power of Jesus' sacrifice. The burden of guilt is gone, and in its place the blessings of sonship have flooded the soul with forgiveness.

I have found Christ to be a companion, guide, and source of strength. This fact is very real to me. I am more interested in getting help to live this day than in inheriting a "many-mansioned" home when life is over. I am not proud of that; I'm just stating a fact. I wish every person could realize what faith in Christ could do for him as he faces the problems and the sorrows of life.

I know many people who have been discouraged and have then looked to Him and found new strength. I covet for every friend that same consciousness of Christ as a companion, guide, and source of strength.

No one can look at the world today and observe its tragic disillusionment and degradation without being driven to the conclusion that man needs a transforming power outside himself to lift him to the planes for which he yearns. Jesus Christ is that power! I have found Him sufficient, adequate, reliable.

I hope that Christ means all of this to you. If not, I can make a few suggestions: Christ will mean little to you if your attitude of self-sufficiency and self-importance dominate your life. If you want Him, He will come to you, but you must open the door. You must invite Him in, not as a guest but as a sovereign. "I will come in to him and will dine with him, and he with me" (Revelation 3:20). If you will take Him as your Savior, He will take you as His own. If you will surrender to Him, He will surrender the joys of serenity and contentment to you. All you ever wanted life to mean to you can be yours as you discover it through Jesus Christ.

PRAYER: "Precious Lord, I believe that Jesus Christ has come in the flesh, was dead, has risen, and is coming again. I confess Him as Lord and Saviour of my life and by faith I accept the challenge of change He offers freely to my life. Make me a clean and useful tool in Your plan that I might redeem the time before time is no more. In the Name of Christ. Amen."

How to get up in the A.M.—
"Lord, I believe!
Lord,
I believe!
Lord, I believe!"

37

THE WORK OF WINNERS

The Lord will be with me, and I shall drive them out as the Lord has spoken.

Joshua 14:12 TLB

Caleb said, "We are well able to overcome them." One of the deepest marks of a winner is the attitude of winning in his work. Work and the winning attitude are the legs which carry the man to his goal.

The work you are doing is suited to your special abilities; if not, then create the work-pattern that is. Once you create the work-pattern you will discover the ability usually follows to carry it out. It becomes a labor of love.

Each time you feel the success-sensation in your work, you will be developing a love for your work at the same time. It's the love of your work which makes you a winner. I have yet to see a true winner who did not develop a love for his work.

He who prepares the work for the worker prepares the worker for the work. Believe that! Whenever the Lord gives us a task to fulfill, it is because He sees in us the talents for its successful and happy accomplishment, as it is done with His help.

Caleb faced difficulties and delays, yet he kept his eyes on the project. It is a serious mistake to turn back when facing head-on difficulties. You just might turn back at the moment of success. Let this become your motto: "It's too soon to quit."

It is a wise man who brings all his resources to God's power and, together with Him, works to win. The Lord who made you can make the most of you. Hand yourself over to the Creator. When He put you together, He did it for you to succeed under His guidance. The "big life" can only come to the top as you yield to Him from the bottom. The abundant life can be yours.

Caleb said, *"We* are able to overcome *them."* Look at the italics: *"We—them."* There will always be something or someone for you to overcome. You are pitted for progress. One would never know the miracle of God if he never had the impossible to face. Let me suggest 5 steps in the work of the winner: (1) Plan your work today for today. (2) Let your heart rest in peace as you go about your work. (3) Avoid the self-appointed providences of other people in your life's work. (4) Know that what you are doing is right, good, and helpful. (5) Always keep in mind that, "There are more with us than are with them."

There is every reason in the world for you to win in life's work. Work like a winner. Who can tell? You may be one!

PRAYER: "Heavenly Father, by faith I lay hold of the surety of Your promise and rededicate my life to Your service. Do something new in me today. Enlarge my concept, expand my mind to greatness through Christ and revive my awareness of Your ability. In the Name of Jesus I can do anything! Amen."

How to get up in the A.M.—
"Good Morning, Lord!
I love You!
What are You up to today?
Whatever it is,
I want to be in on it."

38

OLD CLOTHES

One thing I do: forgetting what lies behind and reaching forward to what lies ahead, I press on toward the goal for the prize of the upward call of God in Christ Jesus.

Philippians 3:13, 14 TLB

Why don't you throw away your old clothes! Old clothes, useless or even questionable, should be given away or tossed away if you want to progress in right thinking and right appearance. The Bible says, "Man looks at the outward appearance" (I Samuel 16:7). Whenever I am tempted to think the outward is not very important, I always go back to that verse and quote it to myself.

The "rut" of poverty is demonstrated by hanging on to old clothes. Don't say you can't afford a new suit or that you can't afford to clean out your closet.

My wife cleaned out my closets. She threw away my old shirts, old suits, and a couple of pairs of old shoes. I feel as if I have started a fresh road to a better appearance. You can't afford *not* to look nice if you want to win. The fear of poverty is the kind of rut that keeps you in hard circumstances. Trust God; He loves you.

Let it become a principle to always wear fresh, clean, and newer clothes. There comes a strength and inspiration to the mind when it is draped in fresh apparel. God clothes all of nature with new garments every season. In the wintertime He wraps the world in the beautiful garments of white. In the summertime He wraps nature in green and many splendid colors. Jesus said, "He clothes the lily of the field, more fair than Solomon and all of his glory." God takes delight in dressing up His world. Think of the millions of colors blended in God's great universe. He made them all.

All of nature believes in the right to new apparel. Each season, Nature discards its old clothes in preparation for new ones. The little animals exchange their garments every season for new ones. Do you think man should do less? Man was made in God's image, so look like it and act like it! If you will make preparation for the new, it will come to you almost automatically.

I have been preaching the Gospel for many years. Each time I step out by faith to enlarge the church, buy new ground, or build a new and bigger building, I have not had the money to do it at the time. But each time I stepped out the need was met. You only have to have a need to get a supply. Not one time will God let you down if you trust and believe. When you make way for the new (because of need) God will always come through.

PRAYER: "Precious Lord, within You lies new life, abundant and free. Help me to perceive the fullness of Christ, teach me to assert the authority You have given me through Calvary by speaking the positive Word of Truth to my situation. Because of Christ old things are passed away; behold, all things become new. In His Name and for His glory. Amen."

The Spirit of truth
within you
makes you alive to truth.
You are in the school
of the Spirit
and there is no graduation.
He makes
everything educate you.
You are alert and alive
to everything and everybody.

39

LET'S FILL A NEED AND FIND SUCCESS

Now may the God of hope fill you with all joy and peace in believing, that you may abound in hope by the power of the Holy Spirit.

Romans 15:13 TLB

There is a formula for success. I suppose there are countless numbers of people who could give their formula for success, if they were asked to do so. The most concise formula for success that I have found is, find a need and fill it. Sounds simple, doesn't it?

If you would search into any successful organization, you would discover that it demonstrated this outstanding formula. They found a need and filled it! All the great leaders of history were those who saw a need, became aware of the importance of filling it, and set out to fill it. These men were alert to the condition or situation of their age and took the challenge to fill the need. Those who fill the needs of others will be the leaders of history.

Happy success is not founded on being smart or clever or using shady practices. Many men have attempted to go down this road but found that it led to disgrace and defeat. These practices may carry a business along for awhile, but eventually the bottom falls out and all is lost. High pressure is a false front for poor salesmanship and poor merchandise. Persuasion built on deceit will end in disaster.

But let a businessman, salesman, or student base his services on sincerity to fill the need of others, and he will soon discover that success is all around him. All of life will see to it that he succeeds, because all of life works with "need-fillers." How many need-fillers can you name in history? Look around you today and see who is filling the need. You will discover that the need-fillers are usually happy and successful. If you are to become the success you desire, find what people really need and fill their need the very best you can. Jess Moody discovered, "Products that sell are those that maintain their quality year in and year out. The death of a product is assured once the quality is cut." When you are filling the need it means you are filling the need in the best possible way year in and year out. This is success!

Many speak of positive thinking, while others talk of positive feeling, but let me add the other half of the formula: you must couple these with positive *action*. Fill the need of others and your life will be crowned with success. When you have something you really believe in, it's amazing what power and conviction will undergird your efforts. What fills the need of others will became a burning enthusiasm in you. Find the greatest need you can fill, and there you will find success.

PRAYER: "Heavenly Father, I want to thank You personally for Your Son, Jesus. I accept Him for my every need. Help me to know, above all else, that Jesus Christ, who died for my salvation and redemption, is also my best Friend, that He is able to motivate my life to success. In His Name. Amen."

*If Jesus Christ
is rightfully presented,
it is almost impossible
to resist Him.*

40

THE POWER OF POSITIVE ACTION

Peter answered Him and said, "Lord, if it is You, command me to come to you. . . ." And He said, "Come!" And Peter . . . walked on the water and came toward Jesus.
Matthew 14:28, 29 TLB

There are many helpful books written today on the power of positive thinking. A new thought to this great idea is the power of positive action. There is no conflict between these two ideas; one seems to follow the other, or at least it should.

I have met plenty of people sitting on the starting line of life with the positive mental attitude, but as far as achievements are concerned they're out of the race. Positive thinking is not enough by itself; it is only half the answer. The full orbit of achieving is *thinking and acting.* It's what I call Attitude + Action = Achievement. To acquire this dynamic characteristic you will need prayer, Bible study, and practicing God's promises. One of the first lessons you need to learn in any endeavor is to keep on doing the correct thing until it works. No one accomplishes much in life who does not practice the power of positive action. Much of our action is cautious action. We move not out of faith but out of fear.

The power of positive action can be seen when Peter walked on the water. The rest of the disciples sat in the storm-tossed boat. Peter began to sink, but not until he first walked out of the boat onto the water with positive action. He at least proved it could be done! I would rather be a wet disciple, attempting

139

positive action, than a dry disciple who never got the thrill of being rescued by Jesus.

It is impossible to estimate the power of positive action. I would expect that many of us have lost untold thousands of dollars and perhaps opportunities for rich experiences because we failed to follow positive thought with positive action. The greatest source for positive action is divine energy. All through the Bible is the powerful emphasis of the winning life, that vitality and power of abundant life. Many have missed this thought and in return have turned multitudes away from the Gospel. Our churches are empty, not because people don't want God, but because the church fails to present Christ in the positive action of His life. Jerry Falwell, pastor at Thomas Road Baptist Church in Lynchburg, Virginia, emphasized this truth by saying, "We are attempting to reach the nation for Christ through a super-aggressive local church. It is the super-aggressive church which presents Christ in a positive reality!" It gets positive results, too! I want you to have a positive mental attitude plus the power of positive action today. Then watch the achievement of your life soar to reality.

PRAYER: "Heavenly Father, I love You; I love the work of Your hands, I love Your church, the body of believers. I decree success for Your ministry in the earth through the power of the shed blood at Calvary and confess that I am willing for the positive action it takes to carry along the work of the Living Christ through my life. In His Name. Amen."

Determine not to bear things
but to use them.
Everything is useful
and needful that He sends.
Nothing is necessary
that He withholds.

41

THE ZIG-ZAG PATH

Just as the Father has loved Me, I have also loved you; abide in My love.

John 15:9 TLB

There is a strong statement in John 11:5, 6 which says, "Jesus loved Martha, and her sister, and Lazarus. When therefore He heard that he was sick, he stayed then two days longer in the place where he was." This family was in a desperate situation. The brother, Lazarus, was sick unto death. The sister sent a hurried call for guidance and help, but the call was ignored and death marched into the home. Lazarus was dead and buried. With all hope gone, what else was there to do but to mourn? The zig-zag path looked as if God didn't love Mary and Martha. Yet Christ did love, and that's why He lingered. What an apparent contradiction! What a perplexing riddle! Why didn't Jesus hurry to the home which was stricken with this fatal disease? Because He had a greater miracle for the family.

Love often deals in ways which seem harsh or cruel. Yet we may rest assured that for Christ to delay His going to the sisters was an act of deep love. Let me hasten to say that many times the zig-zag path on which you travel is not an indication of the lack of direction in your life or a lack of love from God for your life, but it is the only way to the mountaintop.

Repeated afflictions come not as scars on the already-scarred tree, but as the blows of the sculptor on the marble rock. The blows constantly add beauty and value to the marble. God's great desire for you is to be like Him.

One philosopher said, "He is the final dream of all men." The zig-zag path over which He takes us, or comes to us, may perplex us at times, but trust His mind. God makes no mistakes with you; He has your best interest at heart. He seeks to lead you from the paths of destruction, hopelessness, and death. There may be times when all these forces seem to be turned loose on you. You may question God's deep interest and care for you, but remember, if He seems to come late it is because there is a greater miracle He wants to perform in your life.

Which was greater for the sisters of Lazarus: the healing of their brother, or the raising of him from the dead? You know the correct answer! The zig-zag path may puzzle you at times, but keep praying, keep working, keep trusting until He comes. When He comes He brings with Him the power to perform the desires and longings of your heart. The next time you feel you are on a zig-zag path, just keep in mind that this is the best method in climbing the highest hill.

PRAYER: "Heavenly Father, I yield to Your great love. By faith I open my heart wide to Your Spirit. Expand my consciousness of Your ability until I can see the miracle around me. Spoil me so that I'll never settle for less than the abundant, victorious life offered to me through the shed blood of Jesus Christ. In His Name. Amen."

*To conquer
adverse circumstances,
conquer yourself.
To accomplish much, be much.
In all cases
the doing must be
the mere unconscious expression
of the being.*

42

MANAGING PEOPLE CAN BE FUN

Everywhere we go we talk about Christ to all who will listen, warning them and teaching them as well as we know how. We want to be able to present each one to God, perfect because of what Christ has done for each of them.

Colossians 1:28 TLB

An outstanding trademark of almost every successful person is the ability to handle people effectively. Sounds easy, doesn't it? These people may be your children, wife, or husband, or it may be the man on the job. What should you know about managing people? This is a very important question.

The ability to get average people to do superior work is a rare quality in any leader. To have this insight into a man's mind takes great skill. This skill must be learned. The most useful home, the most productive business has at its head a manager of people. It is the capability to motivate and stimulate others to increase production out of respect and admiration for you as their leader.

Dr. Owen Young said, "The man who can put himself in the place of the other man, who can understand the workings of other minds, need never worry about what the future has in store for him." Working with people can be fun if you put yourself in their place. You must seek to see through the other person's eyes and yet motivate him to greater achievement, and at the same time make him believe it was his own idea.

I find that one of the greatest motivating factors in getting people to do what I want them to do is to get them to do it for their own advantage and not mine. If a person can be shown that he is benefiting himself by making a decision or producing a product, he most likely will do it for you and yet at the same time gain for himself in doing so. It was Andrew Carnegie who said, "The able leader is a man who can train assistants more capable than himself."

William James put it this way: "The deepest principle of human nature is the craving to be appreciated." When you have trained other people to become more capable than yourself and can still appreciate them, that's a mark of a winner. People will follow you into any undertaking if they know you love and appreciate their accomplishments. Praise the performance and the performer will do even better.

Managing people can be fun. Put fun into your home-management, your work-management, and your world-management. It's easy to follow the person who puts joy in all he does. Have a relaxed atmosphere that seeks for definite results. Learn the skill to lead people and you have accomplished one of life's greatest secrets to success.

PRAYER: "Lord, Your world is so great, and the fact that You care about me so very much makes me feel individual, totally alive, fulfilled. Help that confident inner self to show through to others, making them desire the Living Christ in the same personal way I am privileged to know You. In the Name of Christ. Amen."

Claim big things!
Claim great things!
Claim joy, peace,
freedom from care.
Joy is infectious.

43

GIVE THE OTHER PERSON RECOGNITION AND REAP THE DIVIDENDS

I . . . please all men in all things, not seeking my own profit, but the profit of the many, that they may be saved.

I Corinthians 10:33 TLB

William James, the great psychiatrist, said, "The deepest principle of human nature is the craving to be appreciated." Even the person who asks for criticism or suggestions for improvement is, in reality, looking for recognition and appreciation. The Bible tells you, "In honor prefer one another." It is a chief mark of successful people to take delight in honoring one another. The self-confident do not fight for recognition, they gladly give it to others. This is one reason they are self-confident people.

The most powerful motivating force in the world is personal praise. This is not the same thing as cheap flattery. If a person works faithfully for his family and employer and receives no personal recognition, dullness and lack of productivity will mark his life. No encouragement means less effective performance.

Not very many of us do a better job merely because we are expected to do so or even are paid to do so. Money is not the best motivation—at least not for long.

When you appeal to a person's self-respect, his ego, you are appealing to the most dynamic force in his life. Man has climbed to the highest degree of success and has fallen to the lowest degree of failure because his ego-appeal was or was not awakened by someone at a strategic time in his life. The serpent said to Eve in the Garden, "Eat and be as gods." Her ego was appealed to. She ate! The consequences of that act are recorded for you in life's history book.

Encouragement and recognition of a person's accomplishments are as necessary to his morale as sunshine is to flowers. People usually bloom under the sunlight of praise and recognition. On the other hand, people die and wither if they live under the darkness of fear, guilt, and pressure. Nothing in nature grows under pressure. All of nature is in a rhythmical pattern. Let discord come into the home or business and you will find failure waiting to greet you.

Determine today to give recognition and watch the benefits come back to you. A psychologist said, "Discouragement, belittling, and fault-finding produce conceit." Think about that each time you are tempted to find fault. For the next 24 hours, I want you to practice giving recognition to everyone you meet. Let your recognition be genuine and sincere. Watch the benefits come back to you as you give recognition to others.

PRAYER: "Heavenly Father, You are a mighty God. Hallelujah! I shout praise to Your Name for the glory of the completed work of Calvary. I carefully accept the authority won in that victory and ask for wisdom in applying it to my personal life and those lives I touch with Your message. In the Name of Jesus. Amen."

Everything the Devil does,
God overreaches
to serve
His own purpose.

44

YOU NEED A NEW MIND

Your attitude should be the kind that was shown us by Jesus Christ.

Philippians 2:5 TLB

Why is the mind drawn toward depression, failure, and sin? Why is it easy to doubt? I read the other day that, "If you are currently weak and defeated, it is due in large part to the fact that your mind has actually lied to you for years about your real ability, trying to cause you to fail."

It seems the human mind is bent on self-destruction. From our earliest childhood we can remember mind-absorbing fear, hate, jealousy, while at the same time searching for security, love, and satisfaction. This conflict seems to be in each one of us. It really takes effort to keep the mind stayed on God and off the downward pull.

It is clear that we need a new mind—one that is strong, more positive and uplifting. The Bible says, "Let this mind be in you which was also in Christ Jesus." Again we are told, "We have the mind of Christ" (I Corinthians 2:16). Now this is not for theological debate, but it is to be fully accepted and acted upon. The new mind is a gift from God, but you will have to cooperate with its exercise in you.

When this new and better mind takes over, it will bring with it strength, guidance, and a motivated direction for living. You will discover newer insights into your abilities, greater ambition for living, and a sense of self-worth. This new mind will little by little conquer fear and doubt and will control the old mind until it seldom again gives you lasting trouble. Creative achievement is never easy.

This new mind will be like another person inside you. It takes charge, it will put peace in the midst of trouble. Always this new mind will lead you toward hope, optimism, and constructive praying. It is really the mind behind the universe which is being shared with you. You will discover that bigger thoughts are coming to your life as the new mind grows in you. When the new mind in Christ takes you over, you will discover a bigger insight into yourself, into others, and into the world. Notice the phrase, "takes you over," for this is the whole secret to the success of it all. You must be willing to submit your failing, depressed mind to this new and dominating mind. To escape the pollution of life and its unbreakable habits, to erase the lost feeling from your life, you must feel, act, talk, and walk with a brightness never known to you before. This mystery is solved through Christ. Let Him give you a new mind today for health, happiness, and direction for living.

PRAYER: "Lord God, I believe in You today! I believe You have the power to cleanse my life from sin and my mind from negative attitudes and are able to put within me the ability to live beyond small concepts. By faith I "let go" into Jesus Christ. In His Name. Amen."

If anyone kicks you,
your attitude of faith
will cause him
to kick you
toward your goal.

45

LEARNING WITH THE HEART

If any of you lacks wisdom, let him ask of God, who gives to all men generously and without reproach, and it will be given to him.

James 1:5 TLB

Most university professors will tell you to learn from without, that is, by putting knowledge and facts into your head. That is only half right. Teachers seek to cram facts into the heads of their students, hoping to educate, but only discover that frustrations and disappointments many times follow that technique. At times the harder you try to gain knowledge, the further away it seems to get from you. The secret of learning comes from within. It's what I call, "Learning with the heart."

It is my conviction that all the knowledge which the inner mind needs in order to accomplish its goal or purpose will come to me as I patiently go about daily with expectation that the answers will come. When knowledge comes to me which I will never use or need for the completion of my ideas or purposes in life, it will simply not be welcomed at the door of my heart and inner mind. Thus the inner self knows what it needs and will automatically respond to all similar truth wherever it is found. The mind will use it for its own end.

All other truth that comes to the mind will be turned away, for there is nothing within which needs it. Everything you need—facts, answers to your problems—is now here. They are just waiting for your inner mind to tune them in and accept them. Try running facts and figures through the intellect first, and the cold intellect will make them void.

It is believing and then seeing. Jesus said, "The kingdom of God is within you." That's better than having a university around you.

All you need to know is around you today. The answers are pushing against the heart, hoping with childlike faith that you will accept them!

The intellect discovers but the inner mind knows. All the great discoveries of the world were made just in this manner. All tremendous discoveries have been with us since the beginning of time. We never invented them—all we did was to discover them. All the great thoughts of philosophy, science, music, and truth are here in our world today. Man simply plugs into these realities. The wavelengths of knowledge fit his desires and he discovers them!

There is not a thought to be thought, a note to be played, a building to be built but that the knowledge of it is already in existence. The first person to discover it will get the credit.

The Bible says, "Truly I say to you, unless you are converted and become like children, you shall not enter the kingdom of heaven" (Matthew 18:3). Man does not create God; he only discovers Him. It is the child-like faith of man looking into the face of the universe with his heart, which discovers great knowledge not gained from books.

I personally do not believe in the system used today throughout the educational world of grading intelligence by letters. You can't measure the inner mind once it is awakened to its unlimited possibilities.

No problem comes to you in your work or home but that the answer is all ready for your discovery. You must become quiet, childlike, and humble to hear it, receive it, and follow it.

You have only to know what you want. Forget about the answers for the moment and go about your work with a firm feeling that you know the answers will come. Your effort will be rewarded. Suddenly the idea you need for your personal mind will come like a flash of light.

Learning is more than cramming the head with facts. It is listening to the heart speak as well.

PRAYER: "Heavenly Father, as David said, 'I will praise You with my whole heart.' That's my feeling for You today. I bring every situation in my life under the control of the Holy Spirit, and for this day I choose to make my primary concern just abiding in You. In the Name of Jesus. Amen."

If you gaze at Jesus
and glance at evil,
you can't help
being an optimist.
If you gaze at evil
and glance at Jesus,
you can't help
being a pessimist.

46

HOW TO OVERCOME WORRY

Therefore do not be anxious for tomorrow, for tomorrow will care for itself. . . .

Matthew 6:34 TLB

Sir William Osler, who organized the famous John Hopkins School of Medicine, lived a life free of tormenting worry. The principle of his life was established on this thought: "Our main business is not to see what lies dimly at the distance, but to do what lies clearly at hand." He overcame the worry habit by living one day at a time. It was Jesus who taught, "Don't be anxious about tomorrow. . . . Live one day at a time" (Matthew 6:34 TLB).

Anxiety is the number one psychological killer in America. The Bible says, "Be anxious for nothing." Easier said than done, but the habit of worry can be overcome! Lowell Thomas kept these words framed on the wall of his broadcasting studio to combat his worries: "This is the day which the Lord hath made; we will rejoice and be glad in it." It was John Ruskin, the famous writer, who had a stone on his desk with one word inscribed on it. The one word stood out in bold print, "Today!"

Anyone who does not know how to overcome worry dies young. You can add years to your life by whipping the worry habit.

Let me share a very simple formula with you from Rick Goings, president of Dynamics, Inc. His success formula spells ADD: (1) Attitude, (2) Direction, (3) Discipline. ADD joy and success to your life. It is your attitude which means the difference between worry and happiness. The correct attitude toward yourself and your opportunities means advancement in your life. Direction is your goal—and your goal gives you direction. Both help you toward achievement. If you don't know where you are going, you'll be worried each step of the way. Once you have direction, stay on course. Discipline yourself to do the winning thing today which will eventually bring you to the desired destination.

Skyscrapers are built one brick at a time. It is impossible to lay all the bricks of a skyscraper in a day. The bricklayer simply follows the blueprint each hour of each day and the dream becomes reality. It is finished!

One of Mayo Clinic's outstanding doctors made a study of nearly 200 leading executives, averaging 44 years of age. Upon completion of the study he said, "A third of these people suffered from one of the three ailments peculiar to high tension: heart disease, ulcers, high blood pressure." Why? Because worry does kill, as shown by this famous doctor. Worry can cause colds, heart attack, and mental breakdown.

I want to offer you five helpful suggestions from Dale Carnegie to use when facing a problem that worries you: (1) Ask what the problem is. (2) What is the cause of the problem? (3) What are the possible solutions to this problem? (4) Which solution do I accept? (5) When shall I put the solution into action? There you have five secrets for overcoming worry.

PRAYER: "Heavenly Father, today is the day that You have made; I will rejoice and be glad in it. Thank You that I am not confined to inadequacy or bound to unhappiness. By faith I take my rightful position in the body of Christ and release the Holy Spirit to work in my situation. In the Name of Christ. Amen."

We learn how to suffer
by accepting suffering
as coming from God
with a purpose of love.
With this faith we can
make adventure out of adversity
and have a peace and praise
which swallow up pain.

47

WHAT MAKES A CHAMPION?

Thanks be to God, who gives us the victory through our Lord Jesus Christ.

I Corinthians 15:57 TLB

A reporter asked Tom Landry, the most winning coach in football, "What makes a champion?" His answer was power-packed. He said, "A champion is simply someone who didn't give up when he wanted to." He went on to explain, "Success is not accidental, we learn how to achieve." Tom Landry further explained the power of positive action by saying, "I'd like to list four short steps that I think it takes to be a champion in the field of sports. First, there is faith. It's believing that you can win. Second, I think you must have training to be a champion." "The Cowboys," he states, "work out four times a week. They lift millions of tons of iron every season. We run many miles to win. Third, to be a champion you have to have a goal. All winning teams set high goals. The fourth thing that makes for championship is, you must possess the will to reach the goal you set for yourself. This is probably the most important quality of all champions." There you have Tom Landry's concept of what it takes to be a champion.

Think of winners like Janet Lynn, who practiced 8 hours a day for 15 years to win a bronze medal in the '72 Olympics, or take a look at Chuck Hughes, who, in the fourth quarter of a nationally televised pro football game back in October of 1971, dropped dead of a heart attack while playing to win. His testimony for Christ will outlast even his championship on the Detroit Lions team. Champions do take chances—they run a risk of winning all or losing all.

The great Apostle said, "I count all things but loss to win Christ." All champions have this one outstanding characteristic. The price to be paid for winning is well worth it when the trophies are passed out at the end of the game. We are admonished in the Bible, "Let no man take your crown." It's a long road to championship. It involves training, surrender, discipline, and a burning desire to reach your destination.

I like St. Paul's words when he shouted, "I press on toward the goal for the prize of the upward call of God in Christ Jesus" (Philippians 3:14 TLB). Never be envious of winners. You would be wise to pattern your ways after their successful ways instead of becoming envious of their winning ways. It is foolish to shut your eyes or refuse to observe the marks of a champion because of jealousy. That's like turning off the lights when you are looking for a way out of the dark.

The life of Jesus is your best example of a champion. Follow Him by the power of His indwelling Spirit. What's the great secret of being a champion? It is a desire to win! You can be a champion, beginning today!

PRAYER: "Heavenly Father, deep within me I'm aware of Your ability to be exactly what Your Word says You are—able to reconcile all things unto Yourself. Come, dwell in my life today—reconcile my attitude, my ability, my inner being to Yourself. Help me to present You to others in the reality of abundant life through the power of the Holy Spirit. In the Name of Jesus. Amen."

We learn the practice
and habit of faith
by verbal repetition
of a spiritual truth.
I must believe the truth
and continually declare it.
We are to transfer
our attention
from our human selves
to the one whom we contain,
Jesus Christ.
Jesus Christ.

48

WHAT IS YOUR SECRET OF SUCCESS?

Delight yourself in the Lord, and He will give you the desires of your heart.

Psalm 37:4 TLB

Bob Cummings shares the secret of success as a millionaire. He says, "I've always followed my father's precept: 'Decide what you want, then act with all your heart as if it's already accomplished.' This isn't the same thing as positive thinking or being a go-getter." Bob goes on to comment, "First you have to overcome self-doubt and all the things you have been taught are beyond your reach. Then sit down and write your own scenery (which means you play the part in your mind which you want to be without sharing it with someone else). After that, half of you must live in a dream fulfilled." Bob Cummings continues to share his secret of success by concluding, "Once your dream is written you have to act on your best impulses. That's the essence of success with me. It worked in my life."

If you were asked to present a set of rules for success, what would you say? A Chicago businessman, who is also director of the Better Boys Foundation, recently addressed the young members of St. Paul's Missionary Church in Chicago. The principles for a happy and successful life which he spelled out for his listeners are so complete and applicable to everyone that I want to share them with you, whatever your age. As you listen to these 14 easy-to-follow guidelines, let your heart accept them for your life's success: (1) Believe in yourself. Of all the people on the earth, there is not another person like you. (2) Reach for the stars. Set high standards for your life. Leo Burnett said, "Reach for the stars and while you may never quite catch one, you will never come up with a handful of mud." (3) Always do a little more than you're expected to do. Go the second mile. Try for the extra foot. (4) Do something for somebody else. Find a way to help another human being live a happier and more useful life in this world. (5) Honor and respect your parents. They deserve your love and respect for what they have accomplished for you in life. (6) Be true to yourself. Be honest with yourself even when it hurts. You can't really kid yourself for long. (7) Get involved. Ask what you can do for your world, not what your world can do for you. (8) Keep the faith. Some people will betray you, but keep trusting people. (9) Try your hardest. Never do less than you're capable of doing. (10) Set goals for yourself. Make it a point to decide where you're going and how you're going to get there. (11) Look up to somebody. Identify yourself with somebody that's successful. Admire a true winner in life. (12) Be kind. Kindness costs nothing but pays big dividends. (13) Get more education. Go as far as you can in school and learning. The benefit of knowledge is beyond all description when it's properly used. (14) Never give up! Never give up! You will encounter setbacks along the way. They'll depress you and crush your spirit, but you must refuse to accept defeat.

I have always said, "Never learn to live with failure." Never stop trying, for there's always another way, usually a better way.

Let me leave one more bit of advice with you. Avoid all hate, greed, and lust. Above all, let God show you how to live. He knows, for He is Life. Now go with the LIFE THAT WINS.

PRAYER: "Precious Lord, today I am free! Free in the knowledge that there is no permanent loss for my life. Thank You that I am not bound to defeat and failure, but born to excel in Christ. Use my life to honor and glorify His Name. Amen."

We maintain deep hurts
because
we won't believe
and praise.

49

WHAT IS DEATH?

Everyone who lives and believes in Me shall never die. Do you believe this?

John 11:26 TLB

The continuation of sorrow in our world seems never to come to an end. Death is always a tragedy. Homes are broken up; the family circle is scattered beyond earth's reunion by death. Habits of a lifetime are snapped; plans and ambitions are scattered to the wind when death comes to any home.

The whole uncertainty of death can either paralyze or prepare us. There are millions who never give death a second thought while there are others who let the very thought of it cause terror in the mind. I don't think God intended for the human race to be overly conscious of death's possibility; nor should we become unconcerned about its approach. One can be taken up with the thought of death until he forgets to enjoy living. Yet at the same time there are many who make no preparations for death at all. For instance, they have made no legal will for the protection of their families and, furthermore, many have not seriously considered the preparation for eternity. Don't let death catch you off guard.

The Bible says, "It is appointed unto men once to die." The question then follows, "What is death?" This question has never ceased to be asked in the minds of men since the days of Adam. Down through the centuries man has asked, "What is death?"

The Greeks were the masters of knowledge in their day. Their love of life, wisdom, and beauty have gone unsurpassed in any generation. Their hearts were even greater than their heads, and yet some of the Greek philosophers said, "The dead are gone forever. Death is the end of all human personality. There is nothing beyond what we see." To picture this dark and cheerless existence of the dead, they chiseled cold granite statues of their dead. With regard to their dead, that was the best the Greek wisdom could produce.

The Romans searched for an answer to death as well. In all their military might and force, organized with rarest of skill, they could not provide a suitable answer to this quest of the human race.

Job, in the Old Testament, asked the searching question, "If a man die, shall he live again?" The Eastern religions say, yes, in some vague form he will live again. The Eastern concept is that man will live again through some animal or plant by reincarnation. What joy this concept brings is beyond my mind. Coming into the world by reincarnation and never knowing who I will be or what I will be only leaves me in the hands of fate!

The candle is snuffed out at death. The breath is taken away. The tears are no more on the cheek nor laughter of joy on the face. The place at the table is empty. The children are no longer greeted by the strong arms of a father or the tender kiss of a mother. The son who bounded through the front door is silent once death has struck. What is this thing called death? It all seems so senseless.

But stop! there is an answer! God sent His Son, who was motivated by love for us, to bring us the unquestionable answer to this haunting quest of the human race. It is all built on history and facts and by many witnesses that there is life after death.

Christ is not a system to accept. He is not merely a good leader of men. He stands out above all others as the uncomparable, unconquerable, living Christ. The Bible tells us death is our enemy. It comes unannounced, unwanted, and unexpected.

It has no favorites—the muddy boots of death walk into the halls of fame as well as the halls of shame. It never asks permission to enter or even makes a bargain. It can't be bought off, it can't be turned off.

But there is hope! Jesus said, "I am the way, the truth, and the life!" He also proclaimed, "If a man die, he shall live again." Christ promised by His own death and resurrection, "If any man believes in me he shall never die."

The question then comes, "Do you believe?" Believing in Christ does more than make you good, it makes you a conqueror. You can face life motivated and death unmoved when Christ is your Lord. He has come to offer the winning life to you.

PRAYER: "Heavenly Father, I feel humble in Your presence today; thank You for being the answer to my life. I open my heart and accept the fullness of Your love and the provision You made for my salvation through Jesus Christ. In His Name. Amen."

God can be
no bigger to you
than
you confess Him to be.

50

MAGIC MESSAGE ON ATTITUDE

I am well content with weaknesses, with insults, with distresses, with persecutions, with difficulties for Christ's sake; for when I am weak, then I am strong.

II Corinthians 12:10 TLB

THE LIFE THAT WINS brings to you the magic message of attitude.

It was a correct attitude and hard work which caused Tom Dempsey, born without a right hand and only half a foot, to kick the NFL's longest field goal, 63 yards, with a specially made shoe. It made history!

Champions are made from right attitudes and a burning desire to excel. There is a way to live every day of your life so that you will be successful each hour of the day. It is not a gift of the favored to be successful. If you have had this idea, get rid of it today. True lasting success can be yours as you develop a correct attitude toward life.

You can have anything in life you really want by growing the proper attitude toward life, yourself, your job, and your objectives. The results will almost be automatic if you follow these simple suggestions: (1) Set your attitude in a correct way. (2) Stay on course once your ship is launched.

It is your attitude which shapes and molds your life. All actions are the direct result of attitude. The reflection of life is in direct proportion to your attitude toward life. What actually comes to you is the effect of your atmosphere, attitude, and action. Attitude is a reflection of self-image.

What you think of yourself will be seen by your attitude. If your attitude is sound, you will succeed at any task you undertake. What makes for a sound attitude? Simply loving what you're doing.

If one is to succeed in his life's ambition, he must love what he is attempting to accomplish more than all the pleasures the world can afford. His achievement means more to him than beating the clock, skipping a day's work, or even planning a vacation. His vacation is his occupation. That may seem different, but all successful people have this love for what they're doing. The very thought of achieving is the payoff for their efforts. Do your best to improve your attitude toward what you're doing. You will discover in return how much personal satisfaction it will bring to you. One of Charlie Jones's secrets of success is, "Get excited about your work." He asks the question, "Are you excited about what you're doing?" The satisfaction from your work comes when you are excited about what you're doing.

Start today to act, look, and talk with the attitude of a winner. It is mental attitude which brings success more than any other single factor in your life. Someone said, "Success or failure in any undertaking is caused even more by the mental attitude than by the mental capacities."

PRAYER: "Precious Lord, I believe in You today. I believe! I believe! I believe! Write Your message on my heart; burn it into my mind until living for You is as natural as breathing, until reacting in faith becomes my natural life-style. Use me to glorify the Father through Jesus, the Son. For His glory. Amen."

The Holy Spirit's fullness
in you
will develop spontaneity,
naturalness,
and fearlessness.

51

HOW TO ANALYZE WORRY

Peace I leave with you; My peace I give to you; not as the world gives do I give to you. Let not your heart be troubled, nor let it be afraid.

John 14:27 TLB

A medical doctor said, "Seventy-five per cent of all patients who come to physicians could cure themselves if they would only get rid of their fear and worry." Fear causes worry. Worry makes you tense and uneasy and affects the nerves of your stomach; it can change the gastric juices of your stomach to abnormal functions and often leads to deadly ulcers. A great many students could excel in their studies if they would learn to analyze their problems and conquer their worries. Potential business people and their businesses would bloom if they would seek to analyze their worries. The hills and valleys of emotional strain bring on ills which cut the motivation drive right out from under you.

Divorce and broken homes are caused more by worry and anxiety than any other single factor. In fact, in our strained society divorce has gone up 80% since 1970, according to the U.S. Bureau of Census. Before you hit the divorce courts or drop out of school, perhaps you should analyze the one big worry in your life. If there is a problem, there is a solution. All important facts of life are hidden under the shell of the impossible. Break the shell and find the answer to your worry problem. You must quiet your mind to successfully analyze worry.

Robert Lewis Stevenson said, "Quiet minds cannot be perplexed or frightened but go on in fortune or misfortune at their own private pace, like a clock during a thunderstorm." Let me suggest three ways to analyze worry:

(1) Get all the facts of the problem which is worrying you. What is causing the worry? You must pretend you are collecting the facts for another person and not yourself when analyzing your problem. This will eliminate too strong an emphasis on self-interest. (2) Seek to quietly and courageously face the facts as you see them. It might help if you would write down all the facts in your favor and all the facts opposing you. Often you will discover that the answer to your problem lies somewhere in between these two extremes. A problem well-stated is a problem half solved! (3) The last step in analyzing your problem is your personal decision and action. I firmly believe in PMA (Positive Mental Attitude), but I also believe in the other PMA—Positive Mental Action. When you start to act on your decision, information and inspiration and insight start to move toward you. The great pitfall in your life is indecision. Experience has proven the enormous value of acting, moving, and getting started. Better to move in a wrong direction than to never move at all. Only moving vessels can be controlled by the helm. Many great ideas have been lost because no one acted on them.

The next time you face a problem, get the facts and then act on your best impulse. Let the chips fall where they will, for you have faced and analyzed your problem and are seeking to do something about it. Analyze the problem of worry and face it head-on.

PRAYER: "Lord God, You have made all things possible to me through the blood of His Covenant. I reach out to You today in trust and love. Do a new thing in me; challenge my mind to grow, my heart to open in love, and my eyes to see the needs of others. In the Name of Christ. Amen."

*The believer
is a participant
of the same power
which the Father worked
in Christ
when He raised Him
from the dead.*